Dr. Jung Young Lee in his book THE *I CHING* AND MODERN MAN introduces the significance of metaphysical and cosmological implications of the *I Ching* in the various areas of contemporary development. He has selected those areas which are not only relevant to modern man, but are also compatible with the basic principles of Change and the *I Ching*.

- Basic Principles of Change in the *I Ching*
- The *I Ching,* a Standard Work of Parascience
- The *I Ching* and Modern Science
- The *I Ching* and Acupuncture
- The *I Ching* and New Self-Therapy
- The *I Ching* and the New Concept of God
- The *I Ching* and Beyond New Morality
- The *I Ching* and New Styles of Living
- The *I Ching* and the Meaning of Death

The *I Ching* is significant to all men and all situations. Dr. Lee believes one must learn to live and to think according to the teachings of the *I Ching* for in it are the beauties of simplicity which will help one live a simple life in a complex society.

Dr. Lee, Th.D. Boston University, is Associate Professor of Religious Studies and Humanities at the University of North Dakota. He is an authority in the interpretation of the *I Ching* in the contemporary scene.

Dr. Lee's earlier book, *The Principle of Changes: Understanding the I Ching,* discusses in detail divination and the psychic condition of man. Both books will be of great interest to all students of the *I Ching*.

THE I CHING AND MODERN MAN:

ESSAYS ON METAPHYSICAL IMPLICATIONS OF CHANGE

THE I CHING AND MODERN MAN:

ESSAYS ON METAPHYSICAL IMPLICATIONS
OF CHANGE

By

Jung Young Lee

UNIVERSITY BOOKS, INC. SECAUCUS, NEW JERSEY

This Book is Dedicated

to

Sue & Jong

PREFACE

In this volume I have made a modest attempt to introduce the
significance of metaphysical and cosmological implications of the
I Ching in various areas of contemporary development. I have selected
those areas which are not only relevant to modern man but also compatible with the basic principles of Change in the I Ching. Even though
the I Ching or the Book of Change has been so widely read by the
general public in the West, its use is rather limited to divination. To
use it merely as a divination book is a grave mistake. Even Hsun Tzu
once said that anyone who knows the book well never uses it merely as
a divination manual. The greatness of this book lies in its profundity of
metaphysical principles, which are pertinent in the development of human
creativities and innovations. In a small way I have attempted here to
restore its lofty image in mainstreams of the cultural and technical
civilization of the West.

The essay on "The I Ching and the New Concept of God" is written
on the basis of my article "Can God be Change Itself?" which was published in the Journal of Ecumenical Studies. I am grateful to the Journal
staff for letting me make use of the article in this book. To aid me in

preparing the manuscript I am grateful to the University of North Dakota for a research grant. I am especially thankful to Jill Gidmark, Rita Kelly and Margaret Fischer, who contributed to the improvement of the manuscript. I also acknowledge my gratitude to Nelda Hennessy for help in typing the manuscript. Finally, I thank my wife and two children whose patience and cooperation made it possible for me to complete this book.

THE TABLE OF CONTENTS

THE I CHING AND MODERN MAN:

ESSAYS ON METAPHYSICAL IMPLICATIONS OF CHANGE

CHAPTER I

ABOUT THE I CHING

Anyone who is acquainted with the I Ching or the Book of Change will recognize that the core of this book is 64 different hexagrams. They are each made of six divided or undivided lines. They are the universal symbols which depict the patterns of inner process which are not realized in actual situations. Thus hexagrams are also known as germinal situations of all possible phenomena. They can be compared with microcosms of all things. Everything in the universe can be reduced to 64 different archetypes in the I Ching. Moreover, each hexagram is unique in its pattern, even though its uniqueness is relative to its relation to other hexagrams. Its autonomy is possible because of its dependence on others. Even though each hexagram represents the complete unit of changing process, it is incomplete without its relation to the rest of the hexagrams. Thus one is inseparably related to others. No one hexagram is in separation from others. This mutual dependency is the basis of continuum in the process of change.

Each hexagram is given a name. For example, the name of the hexagram that is known in Chinese kua ming (卦名), is the most

concise expression that represents the very characteristic of the hexagram. Even though the importance of naming is often forgotten in the
West, it became one of the most important aspects of Confucian teachings
in early days. The name which represents the individual must express
the essential nature of that which it signifies. Thus the name of hexagram conveys its intrinsic characteristics. Just as we are each called
by a name, the hexagrams are also known by their names.

Each hexagram is accompanied by a concise text which is known as
t'uan (象) or judgment. The judgment or decision on the hexagram is
different from the name. The judgment is based on the interpretation of the
very nature of the hexagram, while its name represents the hexagram
without any interpretative function. The judgment is similar to the decision of a judge in court. Just as the court decision comes from a careful
examination of the situation of the case, judgment on the hexagram is
relative to the examination of the hexagram itself. It not only indicates
the condition of the hexagram but the possible predicament of its future
outcome. Judgment is also similar to a doctor's diagnosis which is based
on the condition of the patient. Diagnosis includes not only the condition of the patient but the prediction of its outcome in the future. Moreover, prescriptions are needed to remedy misfortune or undesirable outcome. Therefore, like the court decision or the doctor's diagnosis,

judgment involves more than the analysis of present predicament. It also

attempts to predict the future outcome of that particular situation.

Each line of the hexagram is also accompanied with its own text.

This is often called the hsiao t'uan (爻 象) or judgment on the line.

This judgment is then similar to the diagnosis on the line within the total

situation of the hexagram. Just like the judgment on the hexagram, the

judgment on the line also carries the diagnostic implications. It not only

analyzes the condition of the line but predicts its future predicaments.

The judgment on the line begins with the lowest line of the hexagram and

ends up with the upper line. It is always relative to the judgment on the

hexagram as a whole.

To summarize, the main texts of the I Ching deal with the 64 differ-

ent hexagrams. The names and judgments on hexagrams are merely

intended to represent and interpret them in words (especially in Chinese

words) for our comprehension. In order to understand the I Ching we must

understand the symbolic significance of hexagrams. The I Ching is, then,

none other than the book which attempts to explain the symbolic signifi-

cance of hexagrams in the changing process.

Appendixes to the main texts of the I Ching are known as Shih I

(十 翼) or Ten Wings, which are commentaries to the main texts. The

first and second wings deal with the T'uan Chuan (彖 傳) or the Com-

mentary on the Judgments, which intends to clarify and elucidate the meaning and significance of the judgment on the hexagrams. For example, let us look at the hexagram 37, Chia Jen (家人) or the Family. The judgment on this hexagram says: "The Family. The correctness of woman is advantageous." The commentary on this judgment elucidates it further:

> The Family. The right place of woman (the family man) is inside, while the right place of man is outside. The right place of both man and woman signifies the great righteousness shown in heaven and earth. In the family the parents are strict rulers. Let the father be a father, the son a son. Let the elder brother be an elder brother and the younger brother be a younger brother. Let the husband be a husband and the wife a wife. Then the house is on the right way. When the house is in order, everything under heaven will be firmly established.

Here, the Commentary on the Judgments makes clear the importance of order in the family. In this way the commentary attempts to explain the judgments.

The third and fourth wings deal with the Hsiang Chuan (象傳), which is the commentary on the symbols of hexagrams. This commentary is so important that it is often included in the main texts of the I Ching.[1] This commentary attempts to interpret the structural significance of hexagrams in terms of two primary trigrams. Since all hexagrams are none other than the combination of two primary trigrams, this commentary provides the symbolic significance of the constituting trigrams. Let us take hexagram 6, Sung (訟) or Conflict for an illustration. As we notice

from the symbol of the hexagram, it consists of the trigram Ch'ien (乾)
or heaven (☰) above and the trigram K'an (坎) or water (☵)

    ☰
    ⚏

below. Thus the commentary on the symbols says: "Heaven and water go
their opposite directions. It is the symbol of conflict." Here, the commentary deals with the hexagram in terms of the attributes of two com-
bined trigrams.

The fifth and sixth wings are known as the Ta Chuan (大 傳) or
the Great Commentary, which is also known as the Hsi Tz'u Chuan
(繫辭傳), the Commentary on the Appended Judgments. This commentary
deals with important essays on philosophical and metaphysical implications of the I Ching. It attempts to explain the various questions that
people usually ask about basic principles of the Change.

The seventh wing is known as the Wen Yen Chuan (文言傳), the
Commentary on Words of the Texts. This commentary deals with essays
to elucidate the first and second hexagrams only. It is possible that the
rest of essays dealing with other hexagrams were lost. In the first two
hexagrams this commentary provides a good deal of information concerning

the hexagrams as a whole as well as the individual lines of the hexa-grams.

The eighth wing is the <u>Shuo Kua Chuan</u> (説 卦 傳), the Explana-tion of the Trigrams. This is one of the most important commentaries to the <u>I Ching</u>. It attempts to explain the symbolic significance of the eight trigrams. Let us observe how the commentary describes the attributes of the trigram <u>K'un</u> or earth (☷ ☷). "<u>K'un</u> is the earth, the mother, cloth, a kettle, frugality, level, a cow with a calf, a large container, form, the mass, and a shaft. Among the different colors of soil, it is the black."

The ninth wing is known as the <u>Hsu Kua Chuan</u> (序 卦 傳), the Commentary on the Sequence of the Hexagrams. It attempts to provide answers to the order of hexagrams in the <u>I Ching</u>. Especially the King Wen's arrangement of hexagrams which has been accepted in the <u>I Ching</u> is so random in order that it needs justifications for the arrangement. Why does one hexagram follow the other? This question is attempted to be answered in this commentary.

Finally, the tenth wing is known as the <u>Tsa Kua Chuan</u> (雜 卦 傳) or the Commentary on the Miscellaneous Notes on Hexagrams. It has a brief description for each hexagram. For example, this commentary on the first hexagram, <u>Ch'ien</u> (乾), says: "The <u>Ch'ien</u> is firm." It provides the basic attributes of the hexagram. However, it does not occupy an important place in the Ten Wings.

These commentaries which constitute ten wings are indispensable for the study of the I Ching. The Ta Chuan or the Great Commentary and the Shou Kua Chuan or the Commentary on the Trigrams are especially helpful in beginning a study of the I Ching. They can provide the basic philosophical framework that we need in the understanding of the I Ching. The rest of the commentaries deal with the study of individual hexagrams. They are most helpful in the understanding of the main texts of hexagrams. Since they are an intrinsic part of the I Ching, they can be compared to wings without which birds could not fly. In this regard the Ten Wings are more than appendixes to the I Ching.

Let us now discuss the origin and formation of the I Ching itself. In the Shuo Kua Chuan (説卦傳) or the Commentary on the Explanation of Trigrams the authorship of the I Ching is attributed to the holy sages: "The holy sages formed the I Ching in ancient times."[2] In the Ta Chuan (大傳) or the Great Commentary the same idea is expressed: "The holy sages formed the hexagrams in order to observe the symbols. They wrote the judgments in order to define clearly good fortune and misfortune."[3] Both commentaries attribute the authors of this book to the holy sages or shen jen (聖人), whose names are not provided. According to the tradition, the I Ching has its origin in the most ancient practice of divination and was formally attributed to Fu Hsi (2953-2838 B.C.), one of the great legendary kings in China. It was believed that

King Wen, the founder of Chou Dynasty (1150-249 B.C.), later re-arranged the hexagrams and gave them the judgments or Kua T'uan (卦 象). His son, Tan, who was the Duke of Chou, composed the Hsiao T'uan (爻 象), the judgments on lines to supplement the Kua T'uan or the judgments on hexagrams. If we accept the tradition, it is possible to believe that the holy sages who were responsible for the formation of the I Ching were Fu Hsi (伏 羲), King Wen (文 王), and the Duke of Chou or Chou Kung (周 公). With these sages in mind let us explore more in detail the origin and formation of the main texts of the I Ching.

In view of traditional beliefs we may be able to consider the formation of the main texts of the I Ching in four stages. The first stage might be the most archaic method of divining practice without any reference to cosmological implications. The second stage might be the creation of eight trigrams, which had been attributed to Fu Hsi. In this stage the divination process was closely related to the primitive cosmology. The third stage could be the formation of hexagrams and writing of the judgments which had been attributed to King Wen. Finally, the fourth stage could be the elaboration of the judgments through the writing of the judgments on lines, which was attributed to the Duke of Chou. Let us discuss these in detail.

The I Ching is primarily a divination book. According to the Book of Rites or Li Chi (禮 記), "The ancient kings made use of the stalks of the divining plants and the tortoise shells; arranged their sacrifices; burned their offerings of silk."[4] In <u>Shih</u> <u>Ching</u> (詩經) or the Book of Poetry, divination by means of the tortoise shell is mentioned.[5] It was somewhat later that the divination method by the lineal figures was practiced through the manipulation of the stalks of plants.[6] It was certain that the tortoise shell was first consulted for divination. It was believed that the tortoise possessed the mysterious and oracular power because it survived longer than other living beings. Because of its long life, it became the object of divination. In early days the tortoise shell was incised with a red hot stylus, so that the shell was cracked. The diviner read the lines of the cracked shell to foretell the future. A similar form of divination has been used even in our time in the Grand Ise Shinto Shrine in Japan. In order to select the sacred rice pad to grow rice plants for the sacrifice of food, the Shinto priests consult the divine will through cracking the shell each year. Since reading the cracked shell was so difficult in early days, an easy method of divination was said to develop through the use of a fixed number of milfoil stalks. Because the use of the stalks was easier than the use of the tortoise shell, it is possible that the name of the <u>I</u> <u>Ching</u> or the Book of Easy (易經) might be derived from it. The word <u>I</u> (易) means not only change but also easy. Thus the <u>I</u> <u>Ching</u> was also known as the <u>Chou</u> <u>I</u> (周易). The word "Chou" (周) was used because it was composed by the people of Chou; and "I" (易) because it was an easy method of divination.[7]

The second stage in the formation of the main texts of the I Ching deals with the correlation of the oracle method with cosmological structures in terms of the trinity of world principle. The trinitarian principle includes heaven, earth and man, and is often understood as the Chinese trinity. This trinitarian principle of cosmic process is correlated to the divination process and formed the eight trigrams. The cosmological structure which became the basis of correlating divining process was believed to be derived from the mysterious diagram known as Ho T'u (河圖) or River Map which was on the back of the dragon-horse coming out of the Yellow River. Confucius seemed to believe in it, for he had mentioned it in his Analects.[8] This evidence is also found in the Book of Rites: "The map was borne by a horse."[9] This mysterious chart seems to be a key to the formation of the I Ching. The original map or chart which Fu Hsi received from the Yellow River was believed to be lost in the eleventh century B.C. Later the map was believed to be reconstructed by the so-called School of Five Elements or Wu Hsing (五行) during the Han dynasty.

How could Fu Hsi form the trigrams from this map? It is reasonable to believe that he could have formulated four duograms from this map and then expanded them to eight trigrams through the trinitarian principle of

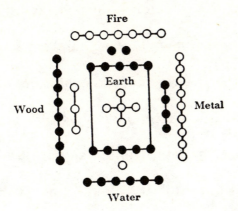

changing process. If we observe carefully, we notice that there are primarily two types of circles: the light and the dark. The light circles represent yang forces and the dark circles represent yin forces. It is possible that Fu Hsi failed to construct the trigrams with circles. Thus he substituted yin for the divided line (— —) and yang for the undivided line (———). Here, all odd numbers became the yang forces symbolized by the undivided lines, and the even numbers became the yin forces symbolized by the divided lines. The circles of the outer side of the map are divided into four groups: two groups of dark circles and two groups of light circles. The group of dark circles which represent water is number six, for it has six dark circles. Another group of dark circles which represents the wood is number eight, because it has eight dark circles. Both six and eight are even numbers representing yin forces. The wood, symbolized by number eight, is lesser yin than the water, number six.

Since yin is characterized by tenderness, water is more yin than the wood. Therefore, the number six which is symbolized by water is known as the great yin or the old yin (= =). On the other hand, the number eight which is symbolized by the wood, is known as the small yin or the young yin (= =). In a similar fashion we have two groups of light circles. The group which represents fire has seven light circles and that which represents metal has nine light circles. Since yang is characterized by hardness, the number seven, which is symbolized by fire, is less yang than the number nine, which is symbolized by the metal. Therefore, the number seven is assigned to the small yang or young yang (= =). The number nine is assigned to the great or old yang (===). Now the four duograms have been attained from the map. They represent the four seasonal changes of the year and the foundation of trigrams. Since these duograms represent the interrelationship between heaven and earth or yang and yin, they necessitate another to complete their relationship. Just as the father and mother complete their relationship in their procreation of their child, heaven and earth complete their interaction through the procreation of man who stands between them, just as a child is in the midst of his parents. Thus trigrams are the inevitable outcome of duograms in the process of change. Because the universe was conceived in terms of organism, every changing process presupposes a procreation. Thus it is said, "Therefore, the I [or Change] is in the Great

Ultimate Beginning. It generates the two primary powers. The two primary powers produce the four symbols. The four symbols produce the eight trigrams."[10] Here, the two primary powers are yin and yang forces, and four symbols are four duograms, which produce the eight trigrams. By adding one more line of either yin or yang, that is, to add a man to the duograms of heaven and earth, we attain the completion of the trinity of cosmic principle. When another line is added to the four duograms in all possible variables, we attain the eight trigrams: Ch'ien (乾) or heaven (☰), K'un (坤) or earth (☷), Chen (震) or thunder (☳), Li (離) or fire (☲), Tui (兌) or lake (☱), Sun (巽) or wood (☴), K'an (坎) or water (☵), and Ken (艮) or mountain (☶). These trigrams are complete units of the universe. In this way the eight trigrams can be easily correlated to the cosmic principle of the trinity.

The third stage of the I Ching deals with the formation of the hexagrams and their judgments. The early tradition attributes the authorship of hexagrams to different sages such as Fu Hsi (伏羲), Shen Nung (神農), Hsia Yu (夏禹) or King Wen (文王).[11] It is possible, for example, that Fu Hsi, who arranged the eight trigrams, was also responsible for the creation of hexagrams. It is generally believed that the different arrangements of hexagrams had existed before King Wen re-arranged them in the present form. The creation of the 64 hexagrams was directly related to the formation of the eight trigrams. Each trigram as the complete unit of microcosmic situation necessitates its counterpart since everything has its counterpart according to yin and yang principle. Thus the trigrams were doubled to make hexagrams. When eight trigrams were fully doubled, that is, 8 times 8, they became 64 hexagrams. Thus the 64 hexagrams complete the germinal situations of the universe. However, the present form of arrangement of hexagrams was generally believed to be done by King Wen, who was also believed to be responsible for the appended judgments. Ta Chuan or the Great Commentary also gives some evidence to support the idea that the judgments were written by King Wen: "At the end of Yin dynasty and the rise of Chou dynasty, the I Ching was given. This was the time when King Wen and the tyrant Chou Hsin were fighting against each other. Thus the judgments of this book often warn against danger."[12] The present form of arrangement and judgments were believed to be done by King Wen while he was in captivity for seven years. As a great diviner King Wen was deeply involved in the arrangement of hexagrams and appending judgments. According to tradition, each hexagram appeared in order on the wall of the prison as a form of vision. In this respect the present arrangement of hexagrams and appended judgments were more than mere products of human wisdom but the revelations of higher reality. Thus the creation of hexagrams and writing of judgments superseded the rational process.

The final stage deals with the formation of judgments to lines of hexagrams. It has been commonly believed that the Duke of Chou, the son of King Wen, was responsible for it. The Duke of Chou was known as a brilliant leader and a great philosopher who could succeed his father's work on the I Ching. He completed the judgments on lines as a tribute to his filial piety, but it is questionable whether he had enough time to devote to the writing of judgments on the lines of all hexagrams. However, it is possible that the work was completed in the Chou court under his leadership. The situations that the judgments had depicted in the I Ching certainly belong to the early Chou period. The traditional name of this book, Chou I (周 易) also suggests that it was originally a Chou manual of divination. Thus we can conclude that the book was completed early in the Chou period under the leadership of a great king, the Duke of Chou.

We have attempted to reconstruct the origin and formation of the I Ching on the basis of Chinese tradition.[13] Those individuals to whom this book was attributed were not alone responsible for the formation of it. Fu Hsi, for example, was a legendary figure who represents the foundation of Chinese civilization. Just as Tan Kun in Korea or Sun Goddess in Japan, Fu Hsi symbolizes the beginning of Chinese civilization. In this respect the I Ching has its origin in the beginning of the Chinese way of life. The formation of the I Ching can be compared with that of the Pentateuch or the five books of the Moses in the Old Testament. Both went through many years of oral transmission and various revisions until they were finalized and written down in the present form. Just as the Pentateuch was originally attributed to the great leader like Moses, the I Ching was also attributed to the great leaders of Chinese history, such as Fu Hsi, King Wen and the Duke of Chou. Just like many national epics, the I Ching perhaps went through various revisions and refinements through the centuries of experiments before it came down to us in the present form. In this respect the authorship of this book belongs to the community of early Chinese people, even though those people like Fu Hsi, King Wen and Duke of Chou were credited to it. It is not only the product of Chinese history but the intrinsic part of Chinese people. Moreover, it has been the source of inspiration and challenge to the Far Eastern people for many centuries.

When we come to the origin of the Ten Wings to the I Ching, we confront serious challenges to the traditional authorship which was attributed to Confucius.[14] Since the sayings of Confucius are available in our time, it is possible to make more critical evaluations of the Ten Wings than the main texts of the I Ching. Since the problems dealing with the authorship of the Ten Wings are often technical in scholarly circles, it is not our intention to deal with the various arguments for or against traditional authorship. We may simply summarize some of the main arguments to show the problems presented in these books.

One of the most serious problems in attributing the Ten Wings to Confucius comes from the contents. As we have already pointed out, the books are collections of heterogeneous writings. Some of them are purely interested in metaphysical aspects of the changing process, and others in the symbolic nature of hexagrams, and so forth. There are not only different interests in the treatment of the I Ching but different qualities in dealing with the problems. For example, the literary quality of ninth and tenth wings is far inferior to the rest of the Ten Wings. Because of their inferior quality of writing, Creel outrageously denies that Confucius had anything to do with them: "These two treatises are extremely brief and utterly superficial; there is no reason to suppose that Confucius would have bothered even to read, much less to write, such trifles."[15] Because of heterogeneity it is difficult to attribute the Ten Wings to a single author. Therefore, it is difficult to uphold the tradition that Confucius was responsible for the writing of the Ten Wings.

Traditional authorship is questioned even in the most highly regarded works such as the Ta Chuan or the Great Commentary and Wen Yen or the Commentary to the Words of the Texts. One of the obvious objections to Confucian authorship of these commentaries is the frequent appearance of the phrase, "The Master said." Here "The Master" is undeniably

Confucius. Confucius could not introduce himself with this formula if he himself wrote them. They must be written by someone else. Creel said, "The words 'The Master said' evidently referring to Confucius; this fact in itself indicates that he was not their author."[16] However, we must remember that this kind of problem is not implicit in the _I Ching_ alone. It also exists in the _Analects_ of Confucius, where the words "The Master said" also appears frequently. Therefore, it is difficult to reject the traditional authorship of these books in the Ten Wings purely on the basis of the phrase "The Master said."

Traditional authorship is also questioned on the basis of the contents of _Ta Chuan_ and _Shuo Kua_. _Ta Chuan_ or the Great Commentary deals with the metaphysical treatise on the concept of changing process, and _Shuo Kua_ or the Treatise with the philosophical aspects of the trigrams. Since Confucius was not interested in metaphysical and speculative philosophy, it is questionable that he had anything to do with these treatises. Certainly Confucius was not interested in cosmology that these treatises attempt to explore. Therefore, this kind of argument seems to support the view that Confucius himself was not involved in the writing of the Ten Wings.

The basic idea of change in the _I Ching_ seems to contradict what Confucius taught in the _Analects_. The _I Ching_ in the Ten Wings teaches that the way to know the world is simple. However, Confucius taught in

the Analects that the way is rather difficult. He taught that knowledge or
wisdom is a hard thing won through discipline and study. Therefore, it
is questionable whether he advocated this kind of simple and easy method
of knowing the truth.

It is also claimed that Confucius did not believe in divination.
Since the I Ching is primarily a divination book, Confucius denounced it.
This criticism had its base on a passage in the Analects:[17]

> The Master said, "The people of the south have a saying--a
> man without constancy cannot be either a wizard or a doctor."
> Good! Inconsistent in his virtue, he will be visited with
> disgrace. The Master said, "This arises simply from not
> attending to the prognostication."

However, it is difficult to conclude that Confucius in the above statement denounced divination or prognostication. The most important statement that "Inconsistent in his virtue, he will be visited with disgrace"
(不恒其德或承之羞) is a direct quotation from the text on the
third line of hexagram 32, Heng (恒) or Consistency. However, Confucius certainly denied the misuse of divination when he said, "This
arises simply from not attending to the prognostication." Therefore, it is
difficult to conclude that Confucius really denounced the I Ching on
account of divination.

This idea can be pursued further. If Confucius really denounced
divination, it would have been impossible for him to say the following in
his Analects: "The Master said, 'If some years were added to my life, I

would give fifty to the study of the I Ching, and then I might come to be

without great faults'" (子日加我数年五十以學易可以無大過矣).[18]

This statement seems to endorse his interest in the I Ching. However,

those who believe that Confucius denounced the practice of divination

argue that the present text of Analects, which contains the word "I" (易)

or I Ching, does not conform to the Lu text in the Ching Tien Shin Wen

(XXIV, 8a), where the word "亦" is used instead of "易." The altera-

tion of this character changes the meaning of the passage. This kind of

textual criticism often goes too far to be in tune with the original intent

of the text. It is difficult for the common people to believe that the

I Ching became one of the important classics of Confucius if Confucius

did not believe in it. Moreover, the I Ching became one of the most

important books for the development of Neo-Confucian movements in the

later period.

We can conclude, from some of the evidences we have pointed out,

that it is difficult to affirm the traditional view that Confucius was respon-

sible for the writing of the Ten Wings. There are many problems to be

resolved if the traditional authorship is acceptable. However, it is

going too far to say that "Confucius had nothing whatever to do with the

Book of Changes."[19] Even though many evidences go against the Con-

fucian authorship, we also find that there are enough evidences to sup-

port the view that Confucius was genuinely interested in the I Ching.

Confucius seemed to respect the Duke of Chou, who completed the texts of the I Ching. In one of his sayings Confucius said, "Extreme is my decay. For a long time, I have not dreamed, as I was wont to do, that I saw the Duke of Chou."[20] He wanted to see the Duke of Chou again in a dream before his death. His respect for the Duke of Chou, who completed the I Ching, seems to indicate that he did not denounce the I Ching because it was a divination book. But even though he might have been interested in it, it is difficult for us to believe that he actually wrote the Ten Wings to the I Ching. There are so many odds against this kind of assumption. It is reasonable to believe that the actual edition of the Ten Wings might have been done by his disciples in the latter part of Chou or in the early Han dynasty and thus have been attributed to their master, Confucius. This kind of hypothesis makes sense in view of what we have discussed so far as to the origin of the Ten Wings.

CHAPTER II

BASIC PRINCIPLES OF CHANGE IN THE I CHING

The central idea that governs the I Ching is no doubt the concept of
I or Change itself, since Ching (經) simply means a classic or a book.
Therefore, let us approach the basic concept of changing process from
the etymological significance of I (易). Unlike a phonetic language
Chinese is pictographic. Thus an etymological approach seems quite
congenial to our understanding of its meaning. The word "I" was
believed to be derived from the archaic pictogram that looks like this:
易 . It has a round head, a sinuous body and a number of legs. Thus
its original meaning was "lizard" in an old Chinese dictionary.[1] The
lizard was believed to move easily from one place to the other and
change from one situation to another. Moreover, the lizard was thought
to change its color twelve times a day. Because of its changeableness
the word "I" was believed to have been adopted for the I Ching. Moreover, the lizard cannot only easily cut off its tail from the body whenever necessary but also easily grow the tail to the body in time-being.
As we will notice later, the cardinal principle of changing process is
based on the detachment and attachment or separation and union of lines.

Therefore, the lizard which can detach and attach or separate and unite

the tail can become the most desirable symbol of Change or I in the

I Ching. The archaic pictogram of this word, that is, "lizard," then

intended to signify the changeableness of circumstances and the easi-

ness of separation and union.

   Another etymological approach is based on the word "I" (易)

itself. It can be analyzed into two different words: " 日 " which means

the sun, and " 勿 " which means "to give up." However, the word " 勿 "

was believed to be derived from the old form of " 月 " which means moon.

Therefore, it is possible to believe that the word 易 was the combina-

tion of 日 and 月 or the sun and the moon. Thus the Great Commentary

said, "When the sun goes, the moon comes; when the moon goes, the sun

comes also. Through the alteration of the sun and moon the light is pro-

duced."[2] Sun and moon like the heaven and earth are two fundamental

forces which rule the world. The sun governs the day and the moon

governs the night, so that day and night are mutually interrelated. The

day represents the light and night the darkness. The former is symbolized

by yang and later symbolized by yin. In this way the concept of yin and

yang or dark and light principles are brought together in the idea of I or

Change. Thus it is said, "One yin and one yang are called the way [of

Change]."[3] Just as the word "I" consists of both sun and moon, the principle of Change involves yin and yang which are bases for all processes of becoming.

Our entymological approaches to the I or Change in the I Ching seem to confirm one of the well known apocryphas, I-Wei Ch'ien tso-tu. According to it, the I has three distinctive meanings: I Chien (易簡) or easy and simple, Pien I (變易) or transformation and change, and Pu I (不易) or changelessness.[4] These three characteristics of I or Change are mutually interrelated. If we observe carefully, all of these three have the word I (易) in common. Because it is common to all of three definitions, they are mutually interdependent. If we put them together, we can summarize the meaning of Change as simple, transforming, and changeless. These are the basic characteristics of changing process.

First of all, Change is simple. As it is said, "The Ch'ien [Heaven] knows through the easy. The K'un [Earth] does things through the simple. It is easy, because it is easy to know. It is simple, because it is simple to follow. He who is easy to know makes friends. He who possesses friends can endure forever, and he who performs good works can become great. To endure is the power of the sage, and greatness is the affairs of the sage. By means of the easy and the simple the laws of the whole world are known. When the laws of the whole world are known, the sage makes his position in the middle."[5] The easiness of Change is the counterpart of the simpleness of Change, because the former is

possible because of the latter. Just as heaven is the counterpart of

earth, the easy, the way of heaven, is the counterpart of the simple, the

way of earth. Heaven changes easily because earth responds simply.

Just as heaven and earth are the bases for all things in the universe, the

easy and simple are ways to change all things. The simplicity of change

is due to the pure receptivity of earth or K'un and it is easy because of

the direct and undistorted action of creativity of heaven or Ch'ien. What

is easy and simple is then pure and direct. Purity is the characteristic of

receptivity and directness is the characteristic of creativity. Pure recep-

tivity and direct action change all things. Thus the way of Change is

easy. If we observe the hexagrams which represent the microcosms of

the universe, their changes are due to the slight change of a line in them.

The change of yin line (— —) to yang line (———) or yang line to yin line

is the basis of all changes. It is the slight transference of a line from

the divided to the undivided or from the undivided to the divided that

changes all things in the world. All changes in the universe result from

the union and division of lines of hexagrams. This idea is implicit in the

archaic pictogram of I as the lizard, which can easily cut off its tail as

well as simply grow into it. To divide and to unite are the most simple

ways to change things in the world. This kind of changing process is

analogous to changes in sub-atomic structure where the change results from the emission and addition of quantum. There is no more easy method than to divide and unit lines in the process of change. That is precisely why the changing process in the I Ching is simple.

The second characteristic of Change is the way of transformation. Change is more than a mere movement or rearrangement of existing elements. Change is transformation, which is to be understood as "transformation." It means to procreate new formations. It is the process of renewal and reproduction. Change is then always accompanied with the new creation. Change is the foundation for all production and reproduction as well as growth and decay. Change is therefore more than action. It is the power to transform and recreate all things in the universe. Things can grow and decay, produce and reproduce, because Change has the quality of transformation. Energy becomes mass and mass becomes energy because of this quality. Without the characteristic of transformation Change does not have power. Change makes the world alive because of this power of transformation. Without it the world is a dead entity. It cannot be the living organism where Change is not active. Because of the power of transformation Change is eternally in process.

Finally, the basic characteristic of Change is also Changelessness, which must be understood as the background of changing process. Change presupposes changelessness. Thus the classical definition of Change is "Change that is also changeless." This paradoxical nature of Change is clearly expressed in the <u>Tao</u> <u>Te</u> <u>Ching</u> (道 德 經), which is Taoistic

scripture par excellence. It is said, "'Being-for-itself' is the all-

changing-changeless. To understand the all-changing-changeless is to

be enlightened . . . . The all-changing-changeless is all embracing."[6]

This "all-changing-changeless" is a paradoxical word which is known in

Chinese as <u>Ch'ang</u> (常). <u>Ch'ang</u> is also translated "Constant, perma-

nent, unceasing, eternal, etc., i.e., the opposite of changing . . . .

<u>Ch'ang</u> is what is unchanging in all changes."[7] The real paradox of

changing process in the <u>I</u> <u>Ching</u> is that Change itself has the unchange-

able quality. This unchangeable nature within Change expresses itself

in the constancy and invariable order of changing process. The water

never flows from lower to higher ground, the sun never rises from the west,

the moon never goes against the sun. The constancy and invariableness

of changing process are clearly expressed in the very word of <u>I</u> (易)

which deals with the interrelationship between the sun (日) and moon

(月). Their relationship is the prime example of the constancy and

regularity of changing process. Thus it is said, "The sun and moon

acquire heaven and shine constantly. Thus the four seasons are regu-

lated and produce all things . . . . When this constancy is understood,

the nature of heaven and earth and all things are known."[8] Again we

notice a similar saying:

Heaven and earth show that docile obedience in connection with movement, and hence the sun and moon
make no error (in time), and the four seasons do not
deviate (from their order). The sages show such docile
obedience in connection with their movements, and
hence their punishments and penalties are entirely just,
and the people acknowledge it by their submission.[9]

This constant and irreversible order of changing process reflects the

changeless element within change. Because Change is also changeless,

constancy and regularity are sustained in all changing phenomena.

Change is the primordial cause and foundation of the changing

world. Nothing is permanent because Change is the underlying force of

all existence. Thus the sun and moon change their direction. When the

sun reaches its zenith, it begins to decline. When the moon is full, it

wanes again. Trees grow and decay, men are born and die, and things

come and go, because of Change. Everything changes one way or

another, because Change is the foundation of all things. Nothing stays

the same. From the macrocosmic structure of the solar system to the

microcosmic motion of orbital electrons in the magnetic field change is

active. One of the most common symbols of changing phenomena is the

flowing water. The universe can be compared with the running water.

Thus Confucius said, "Like the river everything is flowing on ceaselessly,

day and night."[10] Like the running water things don't stay the same. The

ever-changing cosmos is conditioned by Change, which is the source of

relativity and transition.

These cosmic changes reflect the inner process of Change which is the eternal reality. Just as symbols reflect their inner meanings, changing phenomena are also conditioned by the inner patterns of Change, which deal with yin and yang interplay. Thus it is said, "The way or Tao [of change] is known by yin and yang."[11] Since everything changes, everything deals with the yin and yang relationship. Yin and yang are universal counterparts: they are the universal symbols of opposites. Because of this relationship everything has its own polarities. When there is right there is wrong. When there is good, there must be bad. When there is unity, there must be division. When there is movement, there must be rest. Polarities are the basis for all that exists in the world. One does not exist by itself but always with its counterpart. Thus yin presupposes the existence of yang, just as yang presupposes yin at the same time. Yin is the universal symbol of the female, tenderness, responsiveness, earth, cold, etc., while yang is the counterpart of yin, representing the universal symbol of male, firmness, creativity, heaven, warmth, etc. They are everywhere and everytime. As Ch'eng I (程頤) in the Sung dynasty said, "There is only one system of action and response. What are called yin and yang are everywhere. Take, for example, the front and rear. The front is yang and rear is yin. Or take two sides. The left is yang and the right is yin. Or again take the above and below. The above is yang and the below is yin."[12] Thus, yin and yang deal with the entire dimensions or four dimensions of existence. As Royce once said, "Opposition [counterpart] may well be a necessary step in search for the whole truth."[13]

The essence of yin and yang relationship is not conflicting but complementary. Their complementary relationship is clearly manifested in their origin. Their relationship originally came from the northern and southern slopes of a mountain. The northern slope of a mountain where the sun is shaded came to be known as yin (陰), which literally means "overshadowing." On the other hand, the southern mountain slope where the sun always shines came to be known as yang (陽), which literally means "brightness." Since it is the brightness that casts its dark shadow and the darkness that makes bright light shine, both yin and yang are mutually interdependent and complementary to each other. Yin does not exist without yang, just as yang does not exist by itself without yin. Even though yin and yang are the bases for all opposites, they are not in conflict. They complement each other, because they mutually coexist together. In other words, yin has yang in itself, just as yang has yin in it. What is yin is also yang, what is yang is also yin. They are one but two different forms. The complementary relationship of yin and yang is precisely based on this relationship, that is, the relationship between one and two. One and two are not separable, because they are essen-tially united. One represents the ultimate reality, the Change or Tao, and two represents yin and yang. Because one is none other than two, the latter is always inclusive. Thus the basic relationship of "two in one" and "one in two" makes all things possible.

Yin and yang in the I Ching must be then understood primarily in terms of relationships that exist between them. Relationships are the bases for our understanding of yin and yang. In other words, yin and yang are not substance in themselves, but descriptive symbols of relationship, the relationship of opposites. Yin and yang are primarily the relational symbols, because their relationship is the basis of the changing process. If yin, for example, has its substantial being in itself, it can exist by itself. However, in the I Ching yin does not exist by itself, but exists only in its relation to yang. Yang here is the essential element for yin. Likewise, yang exists only in its relation to yin. It is the relation that defines the existence of yin or yang. The primary function of yin and yang is none other than to provide the relationship of universal counterparts. This relationship is the complementarity of opposites, for it is based on the relationship of "two in one" and "one in two." "Two in one" signifies the unity and "one in two" signifies the division. Thus yin and yang are primarily the relationship of union and separation. However, the union is possible because of separation, just as separation presupposes union. Thus, Chang Tsai (張載) said that duality is impossible without unity and the unity is impossible without duality.[14] Duality or the "one in

two" is expressed in yin line (— —), which signifies the division or two
in one relationship. Union or the "two in one" is symbolized in yang line
(———), where the division is brought together in union. Thus yin represents the relationship of "one in two," and yang represents that of "two
in one." Just as yin and yang are mutually related, the "one in two" and
the "two in one" relationships are mutually interdependent on each other.
The former does not exist in itself. It always presupposes the latter.
Thus they have the complementary relation of the opposites.

The interdependence of yin and yang or separation (one in two) and
union (two in one) are clearly expressed in the process of change. Yin or
the one in two (— —) always changes to yang or the two in one (———),
just as yang always changes to yin. Thus the basic principle of change
deals with the union of the separated and the separation of the united.
When the separated are united, that is, when two become one, yin
changes to yang. When the united is separated, that is, when one
becomes two, yang becomes yin. Therefore, the basic pattern of change
from yin to yang and from yang to yin is none other than the relationship
of union and separation. This relationship is the basis for the symbolization of yin and yang. Thus, "Union is sure to give place to separation
and by that separation will issue in re-union."[15] The union and separation, that is, the yin and yang relationship, is similar to the relationship
of opening and closing gates of heaven and earth. Just as all changes

are due to the relationship of yin and yang, everything is procreated by heaven and earth interplay. Opening of heaven and earth corresponds to yin (— —), which is open in the middle, while the closing of them corresponds to yang (———), where the middle is closed. Through the process of opening and closing or union and separation the universe is in the process of change.

Union and separation or closing and opening are basic patterns of the changing process. Everything in the world changes according to definite patterns. The idea of opening and closing is reflected in the growth and decay as well as expansion and contraction of external world. Trees grow and decay and things expand and contract because the inner process of change deals with opening and closing or union and separation. Opening corresponds to growth and expansion, closing to decay and contraction. All things adhere to the same rule. When things grow to their maximum, they must contract to their minimum. When they contract in their minimum, they must begin to expand toward their maximum. Everything has its own scope of expansion and contraction. Within the given scope of minimum and maximum limitations, growth and decay take place. The pattern of expansion and contraction or growth and decay is most clearly expressed in the changing process of yin and yang. This pattern reflects in their symbolic process. Yin, the divided line (— —) grows inwardly together and becomes the undivided line, yang. Since yin line is characterized with tenderness, it is called <u>jou hsiao</u> (柔 爻) or

tender line, which grows inwardly like the tender shoot of growing plants.

This inward growth takes place when yin is at its extreme <u>intension</u>. On

the other hand, yang, the undivided line (———) decays and becomes the

divided line. Since the yang line is characterized with hardness, it is

known as <u>kang hsiao</u> (剛 爻) or the firm line, which is easily broken

into pieces. While the yin line pushes inwardly and grows into the firm

line or yang, the yang line pushes outwardly and contracts to become

thin in the middle and breaks into two. The breakdown of the firm line

takes place when yang is at its extreme <u>extension</u>. Therefore, the

division and union of line are due to the extreme intension and extension.

When one reaches its extreme extension, it breaks off. When it reaches

its extreme intension, it grows into itself. In this way, union and separ-

ation takes place. The division and union of yin and yang lines reflect

the basic patterns of change in terms of growth and decay or expansion and

contraction in all things in the universe.

The basic patterns of the changing process in terms of expansion

and contraction are clearly illustrated in duograms. One of their important

functions is to indicate the patterns of changing process from yin to yang

and from yang to yin. Their maximum and minimum degrees of expansion

and contraction are reflected in duograms. The minimum of yin is known

as the small yin and the maximum of yin is known as the great yin.

Likewise, the minimum of yang is known as the small yang and the maximum of yang is known as the great yang. When the minimum of yin or the small yin (☳) expands to its maximum degree it becomes the great yin (☷), which then changes to the small yang (☳) which is the minimum of yang. The small yang expands its maximum and becomes the great yang (☰). The great yang then changes to the small yin again. In this way the patterns of changing process between yin and yang are established. We can illustrate the changing patterns of yin and yang in duograms as follows:[16]

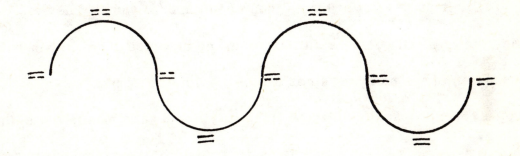

These four duograms express the seasonal changes. The small yin (☳) signifies autumn, the season of minimum cold or yin forces. It changes to the great yin (☷) which represents the peak of yin force or cold. Thus it represents winter. When yin reaches its maximum, it loses its power and yang power begins to expand. Thus the small yang (☳), which follows the great yin, represents spring.

When yang expands its peak, it is known as the great yang (☰) which represents summer. As soon as yang reaches its peak it starts to decline and yin begins to increase. These patterns of change in terms of expansion and contraction are also known as the principle of k'ai ho (開 闔) or expanding and gathering up. When things expand, they gather up. "Where things grow and expand that is k'ai; where things are gathered up, that is ho."[17] The patterns of expansion and contraction or k'ai ho of yin and yang make trigrams possible. Thus it is said, "The two primary forms [yin and yang] produce the four symbols [four duograms]. The four symbols produce the eight trigrams."[18]

Trigrams consist of three lines of yin and/or yang. They are the basic units of all possible situations in the universe. The maximum expansion of yin and yang lines makes the four duograms possible, and the maximum expansion of three lines of yin and yang makes the eight trigrams possible. While duograms become ontological foundations for all things, trigrams become functional units for all situations. Since yin and yang are the basis for all existence, the addition of either of them does not change the ontic nature. In other words, the trigrams are none other than the combinations of yin and yang. What makes them different from duograms is then functional. They represent the functional units of the changing process. Since change presupposes procreation, the interaction between yin and yang lines necessitates another line as their procreative process. Thus trigrams are essential for the continuation of

yin and yang interplay. Because they are essential functions of yin and

yang interaction, they are the complete symbols of changing situation.

They are drawn from the Chinese trinity: heaven, earth and man. The man

who occupies the central line of the trigram is none other than the product

of both heaven and earth, but he is unique because of his position in the

center.

Trigrams are formed by adding another line of either yin or yang to

duograms. They are Ch'ien (☰), K'un (☷), Chen (☳), Sun

(☴), K'an (☵), Li (☲), Ken (☶), and Tui (☱).

Each trigram has its own attributes even though it is a part of the whole

process. The trigram Ch'ien consists of the undivided lines only. It is

the symbol of pure creativity or heaven, while the trigram K'un is the

counterpart of Ch'ien, consisting of all divided lines. Thus, K'un repre-

sents the receptivity and earth. The original meaning of Ch'ien is dry,

while that of K'un is moist. Since the dry is light, it goes up to heaven.

Thus it came to be identified with heaven. On the other hand, the moist

is heavy so it sinks down to become earth. Ch'ien is also the symbol of

a dragon which is associated with thunder and lightning. K'un represents

the mare which opposes the dragon. Just as the mare K'un is gentle and

receptive, Ch'ien, on the other hand, is strong and active. K'un is the

symbol of mother, while Ch'ien is the symbol of father. The former has the black color which is receptive, while the color of the latter is deep red which represents the active character.

The trigram <u>Chen</u> (☳) represents the first son who resembles his mother, for it is the female who searches first for the power of male. The trigram <u>Sun</u> (☴) is the first daughter who resembles her father, because the male first seeks after the power of female. Thus the son usually resembles his mother and the daughter resembles her father. <u>Chen</u> is characterized with thunder and arousing, while <u>Sun</u> is gentle and penetrating. The former is decisive but the latter is indecisive.[19] The former represents bamboo that is straight, while the latter represents wood which grows mellow. The former is dark yellow, while the latter is white.

The trigram <u>K'an</u> (☵), the second son, was originally known in the pictogram " 川 ," which came to be written as " 水 " or water. The trigram <u>Li</u> (☲), the second daughter, is the apposition of <u>K'an</u>, representing fire. <u>K'an</u> is north, <u>Li</u> is south. The former is the symbol of deep water or an abyss, while the latter is the symbol of fire. In the body the former represents ears, the latter eyes. In the animal kingdom the former represents the pig which likes muddy water, and the latter represents the pheasant which resembles a firebird. Both of them are opposite in character but mutually complementary.

The trigram Ken (☶), the third son, is the symbol of a mountain, which is characterized with steadiness. The trigram Tui (☱), the third daughter, is the symbol of a lake, characterized with joy and gladness. As the shape of trigram Tui indicates, it is the joy of the mouth or tongue. Thus she is interested in gossiping. Ken, on the other hand, is the opposite of Tui. It is the symbol of steadiness and silence. Ken is the symbol of the gate keeper who endures long silence, while Tui is the symbol of the concubine who wants immediate joy and regrets later life.

These eight trigrams, which are known as pa kua (八卦), convey various attributes representing all possible situations of the universe. They are correlated with different dimensions of existence as well as different seasons of the year. When these trigrams are doubled, they constitute hexagrams.

Hexagrams are then none other than double trigrams and are known as chung kua (重卦), which literally means double trigrams. When the eight trigrams are doubled in all possible ways they result in 64 hexagrams. In this respect there is no essential distinction between hexagrams and trigrams. Thus trigrams are often described as the hsiao sheng kua (小成卦) or the small kua, while the hexagrams are known as the ta sheng kua (大成卦) or the great kua. What makes them different is none other than the size of kua. Thus the distinction between them is more quantitative than qualitative. However, there is also a quantitative

change for the hexagram is more than the sum of two different trigrams.

Just as the whole is more than the sum of its parts, the hexagram is more

than the combination of two trigrams. In this respect hexagram is unique

from trigrams. Hexagrams are known as the complete germinal situations

of the world. Just like the atoms which have certain patterns of existence,

hexagrams are archetypes of all changing phenomena. They are micro-

cosms of the universe. Thus it is said, "The I Ching [or 64 hexagrams]

contains the measure of heaven and earth. Thus it enables us to conceive

the tao of heaven and earth."[20] Each hexagram, which represents the

basic structure of changing process, is unique but its uniqueness is

relative to the whole hexagrams. Unless each hexagram is to be under-

stood in relation to the whole, it loses its meaning. Just as hexagrams

are interdependent on one another, everything is interdependent in the

process of change.

Mutual interdependency also exists within the structure of the

hexagram itself. The yin and yang lines which constitute the hexagram

are not only dependent on the hexagram but the hexagram is also dependent

on them. When a line changes from yin to yang or from yang to yin, the

hexagram which contains it also changes to another hexagram. Let us

take an example to illustrate the change of a line that affects the struc-

ture of hexagram. Let us look at the hexagram K'un which is the symbol of earth. It consists of yin (broken) lines only. When its first line (always

count from below) changes from yin to yang, it changes to the hexagram

```
── ──        ── ──        ── ──
── ──        ── ──        ── ──
── ──        ── ──        ── ──
── ──        ── ──        ── ──
── ──        ── ──        ── ──
── ──        ──────        ── ──
```

K'un   Fu   Po

Fu or Returning. However, when the last line of K'un changes from yin to

yang, it changes to the hexagram Po or Collapse. When the line changes,

a whole hexagram also changes. Thus the line is intrinsically related to

the hexagram. Moreover, lines are dependent on the hexagram to which

they belong. The dependency of lines on the hexagram can be seen

clearly when we observe the judgments on lines, which are always rela-

tive to the judgment on the whole hexagram. Each line has its place

within the hexagram. Also the function of the line differs according to the

location of its place in the hexagram. It is usually understood that the

second and fifth positions in the hexagram are the most significant posi-

tions, influencing the situation that the hexagram depicts. Lines also

indicate the trends of evolvement in the hexagram. If we take the first

hexagram, Ch'ien, we see clearly the evolvement of lines. The first line

indicates the dragon lying hidden in the deep. In the second line the dragon appears in the field. In the fourth line the dragon leaps up over

the depth. In the fifth line the dragon is flying in the sky. In the last

```
———    6
———    5
—·———  4
———    3
———    2
———    1
```

line the dragon exceeds the proper limits. Here, we notice that each line

indicates its place in the movement of the dragon which is represented in

this hexagram. However, we also notice that the basic patterns of chang-

ing process are also found within the hexagram. When the dragon

increases its strength to its maximum degree in the fifth line, it starts to

decline in the sixth line. In other words, the changing process within

the hexagram also operates in terms of growth and decay or expansion and

contraction. When one reaches its extreme, it must revert itself to its

minimum. These basic patterns of change between yin and yang are found

in the hexagram, because it represents the germinal structure of cosmos.

Everything corresponds to micro-macrocosmic relationship. The hexa-

grams are macrocosms of the yin and yang lines, and the latter are the

microcosms of the former. Moreover, the hexagrams are the microcosms

of the universe. They are the germinal situations where all possible

situations of changing process are inherent. That is why the I Ching, which is none other than 64 different hexagrams, contains the measure of

heaven and earth and enables us to conceive all things.[21]

CHAPTER III

THE I CHING, A STANDARD WORK OF PARASCIENCE

Almost half a century ago the President of the British Anthropological

Association asked Carl G. Jung, "How can you explain the fact that so

highly intellectual a people as the Chinese have produced no science?"

To this question Jung replied, "This must really be an optical illusion,

because the Chinese did have a 'science,' whose 'standard work' was

the I Ching, but that principle of this science, like so much else in China

was altogether different from our scientific principle . . . . The science

of the I Ching, indeed, is not based on the causality principle, but on a

principle (hitherto unnamed because not met with among us) which I have

tentatively called the synchronistic principle."[1] This science of the

I Ching, which is based on the synchronistic principle, is "wider, more

profound, and higher understanding" than the so-called science in the

West.[2] This kind of inclusive science of the I Ching is henceforth

called "parascience."

As Jung had indicated, the key to the understanding of parascience

or the inclusive science of the I Ching is not the causality principle,

with which we have been acquainted in the past, but the synchronistic

44

principle. Synchronisty means "the coincidence of events in space and time as meaning something more than mere chance."[3] It is an acausal connecting principle, which "lies in the relative simultaneity of events, therefore, the expression of synchronistic."[4] However, this relative simultaneity of correspondences is not a sheer chance,[5] even though chance is a means of synchronistic principle. It is a meaningful correlation because it is dependent on time and space. "In other words, whatever is born or done in this moment of time has the quality of this moment of time."[6] Even though it is a meaningful correlation, it cannot be rationalized, because our rational process is based on the causality principle. Its meaning is confirmed by the testimony of experience only, for there is no logical or rational method to verify this principle. The I Ching, which is based on synchronisty, seems to give this kind of evidence that cannot be proven by our reasoning process. Of countless witnesses in the past, Carl Jung appears to confirm the validity of this principle in the I Ching by his following testimony:

> At his first lecture at the psychological club in Zurich,
> Wilhelm [Richard Wilhelm] at my request, demonstrated the
> method of consulting the I Ching and, at the same time,
> made a prognosis which in less than two years, was ful-
> filled to the letter and with unmistakable clearness. This
> fact could be further confirmed by many parallel experi-
> ences.[7]

The reality of this kind of experience cannot be meaningfully related by the intellectual tool which is the basis of the "so-called science" in the

West. This tool is the intellectual process of excluding one from the other. That is why the simultaneity of events cannot be dealt with the "so-called science" in the West.

Let us first examine the intellectual process which is often known as the "Western way of hiding one's heart under the cloak of so-called scientific understanding."[8] As we said, it is an exclusive approach to the understanding of reality, because it makes use of the category of either-or, which is deeply rooted in the Aristotelian logic. As Wilfred C. Smith said, "An intelligent man must choose: either this or that."[9] In other words, to be intellectuals in a traditional sense must be analytic and discriminative through the use of either-or classification. This is an exclusive method because it excludes the validity of the middle between the two extremes of either this or that. In this kind of approach to reality, to be intellectual is to be exclusive. In the intellectual process of the past we discern one by excluding it from the other. In this respect, the sharper the distinction we make, the greater intellectuals we can become. Thus, the either-or way of thinking becomes the crux of intellectual and scientific method in a traditional sense. This kind of method which makes use of the causality principle alone must have been in the mind of Carl Jung when he mentioned the "so-called scientific understanding" of the West. Because of this absolutistic and deterministic categorization of things, it is not possible to assert the simultaneous correlation of opposites. In other words, our rational process does not allow the relative simultaneity of opposite characters. For example, it cannot accommodate both "Yes" and "No" simultaneously. "Yes" is the denial of "No," and "No" is the denial of "Yes" in this kind of intellectual process. That is why we in our intellectual tradition must choose either "Yes" or "No." We cannot have both of them at the same time. What is right must be wrong, and what is wrong must be right. There is no way to allow the validity of both of them at the same time. Perhaps we are the victims of the "so-called scientific way of thinking" in the West.

This kind of intellectual method based on the causality principle alone is questioned in the light of new discoveries in recent science. In other words, the Aristotelian logic of the either-or classification is seriously questioned by the development of the theory of relativity and the new nuclear physics of our time. As a result of these discoveries in the German-speaking countries both Werner Heisenberg and Carl-Friedrich von Veizsaeker had the courage to deny the validity of the Aristotelian logic of either-or.[10] The theory of relativity almost made the claim of any absolutistic statement impossible. According to this theory everything is relative and changing. Nothing is absolute in the world. This kind of relativistic view "gained support from biology on the one hand through de Vries' mutation theory from nuclear physics, and on the other hand through Heisenberg's principle of indetermination and de Broglie's wave theory."[11] With the development of Planck's quantum theory light is no

longer either wave-like or corpuscular, but both wave-like and corpuscu-

lar at the same time. Moreover, it is evidenced that both a particle and

anti-particle co-exist simultaneously.

> Since the discovery of the anti-electron, physicists have
> found--or produced in their laboratories--anti-particles
> corresponding to every known particle. The fifty particles
> known today and their fifty 'antis' are in every respect
> alike, except that they have opposite electric charges,
> magnetic moments and opposite 'spin' and 'strangeness.'"[12]

The co-existence of both particle and anti-particle or both negative and

positive charges seems to be clearly evident. Therefore, it is almost

untenable to hold the view that things are classified either this or that.

We also see that the materialistic determinism which is the basis for the

claim of the causality principle is no longer possible since the develop-

ment of depth psychology and parapsychology. In 1968 Russian scientists

announced their discovery: "All living things--plants, animals and

humans--not only have a physical body made of atoms and molecules,

but also a counterpart body of energy: They called it 'The Biological

Plasma Body.'"[13] The discovery of this counterpart body which simulta-

neously co-exists with the physical body makes the either-or classifica-

tion of our intellection almost impossible. There is no way to assert

either the biological plasma body or the physical body, since they are

simultaneously present in our existence. Thus, the exclusive way of thinking which does not allow the opposites or counterparts to co-exist is limited. That is precisely why Carl Jung implies that the "so-called science" in the West, which is based on the causality principle, is far more limited than the science of the I Ching or parascience.

Parascience, which is based on the synchronistic principle, is an inclusive approach to reality. Since synchronistic principle deals with the relative simultaneity of co-existence, it does not separate one from the other. Rather, it affirms the simultaneous acceptance of both opposites or counterparts. This kind of inclusive approach to reality is based on the idea of the yin and yang relationship in the I Ching. In the process of change both yin and yang are counterparts but do not conflict in their relationship. They are mutually complementary. This principle of complementarity existing primarily in yin and yang is the very character-istic of parascience. Therefore, in parascience both "Yes" or yang and "No" or yin are not exclusive but inclusive. They are inseparable. In other words, in every "Yes" there is an element of "No." In every "No" there is an element of "Yes." No matter how affirmative our answer might be, it includes our negation at the same time. In this way, there is no absolute "Yes" or "No." It is, as Jung said, the relative simultaneity of counterparts. This inclusive understanding of reality must be seen in terms of the "both-and" or "yin-yang" way of thinking.[14] In other words, the synchronistic principle, which is the basis of parascience, presupposes the both-and way of thinking rather than the either-or method.

Let us examine the validity of this inclusive way of thinking as a means of

deeper understanding of reality as a whole.

Perhaps the profundity of this relative simultaneity of yin and

yang, which makes the both-and way of thinking possible, is clearly

demonstrated in the T'ai Ch'i T'u (太 極 圖) or the Diagram of the Great

Ultimate, which was discovered by Chou Tun-i (周 敦 頤), the front

runner of Neo-Confucian philosophy. This diagram is seen all over China,

Korea and Japan in temples, in pieces of art work and in many other

places. This diagram is the very symbol of the national flag of South

Korea. Thus it is also called the flag of the Great Ultimate. As we see

from the diagram, it is a perfect symmetrical symbol of change in which

both yin and yang or darkness and light are mutually intertwined in

harmony. This symbol of the Great Ultimate represents the metaphysical

Yang

Yin

principle of change in the I Ching. Thus, Ta Chuan or the Great Com-

mentary to the I Ching says, "The Great Ultimate is in the I or Change.

It produces the two primary forms. The two primary forms produce the four symbols. The four symbols produce the eight trigrams."[15] Just as

the source of two primary forms of yin and yang is change, the Tao is

also their origin. Thus, it is said, "One yin and one yang are called

Tao."[16] In this respect Ch'u Chai's view is right to identify change or I

with Tao. He says, "The word I is used interchangeably with the word

Tao, since Tao is life, spontaneity, evolution, or, in one word, change

itself."[17] If the diagram of the Great Ultimate represents the concept of

Tao as well as change itself, what is ultimately real consists of both yin

and yang or dark and light together. This diagram attempts to illustrate

the fact that light is not absolutely light but is also dark, because it has

a dark dot. Darkness is not absolutely dark, because a light dot is found

in it. Just as the light principle presupposes the existence of the dark in

it, the dark principle also presupposes the existence of the light in it. In

yang yin is hidden, and in yin yang is hidden. One presupposes the other.

In this regard, it is the symbol for the relative simultaneity of opposites,

which is the basic character of the synchronistic principle. The symbols

of yin and yang are counterparts, but they are complementary for the com-

pletion of the whole.

The idea of complementary relationship between yin and yang is

more clearly and simply expressed in the symbolization of them in lines in

the I Ching. Yin is symbolized by the broken line (— —), and yang by

the unbroken line (———). Everything in the world can be reduced to these two symbols, since yin and yang constitute the ultimate reality. In

the process of change yin or the broken line changes to yang or the

unbroken line, and yang or the unbroken line changes to yin or the broken

line. In this process of change the yin line always changes to the yang

line by merger. On the other hand, the yang line always changes to the

yin line by separation. What makes yang different from yin is a certain

state of existence in which the line is not divided. What makes yin

different from yang is also a certain condition of existence in which the

line is broken. Since the union and separation of line are conditional

factors, they are essentially the same but existentially different. Yin is

none other than the yang divided or broken, and yang is none other than

the yin unbroken or undivided. The broken line is possible because of

the unbroken line, and the unbroken line is possible because of the

broken line. In other words, "Yin presupposes the existence of yang,

and yang also presupposes the existence of yin."[18] Yin is the back-

ground of yang, and yang is the foreground of yin. Since one pre-

supposes the existence of the other, we cannot speak of one without the

other. To speak of yang is to speak of yin and to speak of yin is also to

speak of yang. They are mutually interdependent and inclusive of each

other. That is why the basis of hexagrams is the complementary principle,

the relative simultaneity of opposites. Because of the complementarity of

yin and yang, the basic frame of our parascientific thinking ought to be both-and rather than either-or. Since one is inseparable in any condition

from the other, parascience always presupposes the category of both-and.

Let us examine how this kind of relationship is related to our experience

of life.

Carl Jung is right to say that the science of the I Ching or para-

science is based on the life experience rather than intellectual specula-

tions.[19] The I Ching is based on the actual observation of natural

phenomena of life. Thus, it is said, "The holy sages surveyed all the

possible rules of changes and movements under heaven. They contem-

plated the forms and phenomena, and made the representations of them,

which were summarized in the symbols [of the hexagrams in the I Ching]."[20]

The symbols of yin and yang which constitute hexagrams are then taken

from the natural phenomena that we experience in life. As we have already

pointed out, the original concept of yin and yang grew out of the southern

and northern slopes of the mountain. The southern slope of the mountain

represents the symbol of light or yang, and the northern slope of it is

symbolized by darkness or yin. Using the original meaning of yin and

yang, darkness and light, we can see their relationship in our daily

experience. Since a whole day consists of both light and darkness, it

is possible to illustrate the relationship between yin and yang. When

the sun is at the zenith, light is fully intensified, but when midnight

comes, darkness expands in its fullness. In other words, the maximum expansion of light is called noon, and the maximum expansion of darkness is called midnight. Between these two extremes light and darkness or yin and yang are mutually interacting. However, these two extreme poles are not absolute. Noon is not absolutely without darkness, just as the midnight is not without light. Noon is none other than the most intense light as well as the least intense darkness. On the other hand, midnight is the most intense darkness and the least intense light. In other words, the bright noon must be understood as the weakest moment of the dark principle. Also, the dark midnight is possible because of the weakest form of light principle at night. If we observe the day as a whole, we can notice the co-existence of both the light and darkness. In the morning the dark power begins to lose its strength at the same time the light gains strength. When the sun comes at its zenith, the light gains full strength and the dark principle is at its weakest. As soon as the light principle reaches its full strength, the dark principle begins to gain its strength to overcome the power of light. When the sun comes in the West the darkness gains enough strength to overcome the power of light. When the midnight comes, the darkness becomes its fullest in power. However, at the very moment of maximum expansion the dark principle begins to wane. When darkness starts to contract, light starts to grow. When light contracts, darkness expands. Light and darkness co-exist together. In other words, the difference between the day and night is none other than the degree of intensification between light and darkness.

Their relationship can be best described in terms of the relative simultane-

ity of opposites. They are opposite but complementary to each other.

Darkness is none other than light de-intensified, and light is none other

than darkness de-intensified. Everything changes according to this

pattern of intensification and de-intensification or growth and decay

between the counterparts. When yin grows, yang decays; when yang

expands, yin contracts. They are inversely related in the process of

change. When yang is strong, yin is weak. When yin gains its power,

yang loses its strength. In this way the mutual interdependency is

maintained in the world of change and transformation.

One of the most obvious life experiences deals with sound and

silence. Since most of our thinking process is based on the either-or way

of classification, we don't recognize both silence and sound at the same

time. When we hear the sound of music, for example, we don't notice

that silence is also present in the background. However, when the

music stops, we then notice the presence of silence. It is not silence

which comes after the music. It is not the music which comes from

silence. Rather, silence has existed all along when the music is played.

There is no way to produce sound without silence, just as silence is not

thinkable without sound. Whenever there is silence there is also sound,

and whenever there is sound, there is also the silence as its background.

They are essentially united but existentially different. We know that silence is none other than the sound unvibrated, and sound is none other than the silence vibrated. Thus, we often use the symbol of a straight line (———) to signify the silence, and the zigzag (〰〰) to signify the sound. Silence is then the sound in a different form, just as sound is the silence in a different manifestation. They cannot be separated, because one is not possible without the other. Therefore, the relationship between silence and sound is to be understood in terms of the relative simultaneity of opposites, the synchronistic principle, which is basically the both-and approach to our understanding of reality as a whole.

The same kind of relationship is also applied to our experience of moral and ethical issues. It is difficult to assert that good and evil are in conflict and incompatible in our life experience. What is good and what is evil are relative to certain circumstances. In other words, what is good can be evil and what is evil can be good, depending on circumstances. It is good to kill people in a battle field, but it is evil to kill them in a peaceful town. There is no way to make an absolute classification of our moral and ethical behaviors in terms of either good or evil. It is also true in all other aspects of life. Thus, Lao Tzu describes how every affirmation of this kind gives rise to the opposite affirmation:

In this world, everyone recognizes the beautiful as being
beautiful, and that is why ugliness exists; and everyone
recognizes the good as being good, and that is why bad
exists. 'There is' and 'there is not' produce each other;
'easy' and 'difficult' give rise to each other; 'long' and
'short' exist only comparatively with each other, 'high'
and 'low' are interdependent; there are no notes without
harmony; there is no 'before' without an 'after' to follow
it.[21]

As we have illustrated through various life experiences, essential

truth seems to be in a continuum, the undifferentiated whole. Even

though things seem to contradict, they are not in conflict in their reality.

The conflicting dualism is based on the causality principle, which deals

only with the penultimate reality. On the other hand, the ultimate reality

is seen in terms of a continuum, where dichotomy is overcome. One of

the most clear illustrations is found in the mass-energy equation formula,

E is equal to mc^2, which is based on the special theory of Einstein's

relativity. In this formula we notice that both E or energy and m or mass

are equal when the conditional factor c^2 or the constant (speed of light)

is added. In other words, they are in the continuum but manifest in

different forms because of the conditional factor. Thus, the synchronistic

principle, which is the foundation of parascience, seems to presuppose

the essential continuum in all things. Carl Jung seems to affirm this

idea when he said: "It [the synchronistic principle] seems, indeed, as

though time, far from being an abstraction, is a concrete continuum which

contains qualities or basic conditions manifesting themselves simultaneously in various places in a way not to be explained by causal

parallelism, as, for example, in cases of the coincident appearance of

identical thoughts, symbols, or psychic states."[22] Since the continuum

is an essential aspect of synchronistic principle, the parascientific world

view is more closely associated with the living organism than the

mechanistic view of the world. Everything seems interdependent in the

world of the living organism. This kind of world view seems to become

real in our experience with the ecosystem. The delicate balance and

correlation of ecological system reminds us the failure of the classical

science or the "so-called science," which is based on the static world

view, to deal with the ecological problems. Just as the movement of a

finger is correlated with all other parts of the body, what we do here will

affect other parts of the universe. This kind of interdependence and

interrelation becomes more evident through the development of mass com-

munications and computer technology in our time. The ever-changing

world view of the I Ching through the interplay of yin and yang is not

intrinsically different from the world of relativity and new nuclear physics

of our time. We shall attempt to elucidate further on the relationship

between the I Ching and the development of modern science in the next

chapter. As we will notice the classical science moves toward para-

science which seems to occupy the core of theoretical science in our

time. In this regard Carl G. Jung is right to say that the I Ching as the standard work of parascience in China offers a more profound and higher

understanding of life than the "so-called science" or the classical

science in the West.

CHAPTER IV

THE I CHING AND MODERN SCIENCE

At first glance it seems almost untenable to relate the I Ching, one

of the most archaic books in China, to the development of modern science

in our time. They are apart not only in time but in space as well. The

I Ching grew up in China as a divination book, while modern science

grew out of the rational tradition of the West. From our initial encounter

between them, we notice the great gap between them because of separate

traditions. In introducing the I Ching to the Western world Hellmut

Wilhelm describes the nature of the strangeness and difficulty. He says:

> This book is difficult to understand; it is so full of cryptic
> sayings and seemingly abstruse matters that an explanation
> is not readily available, and we are tempted to fall back on
> interpretation to get at the meaning. To us children of an
> essentially rational generation it poses a problem we are at
> first reluctant to face; we are led into a region in which we
> do not know the terrain, and which we have forbidden our-
> selves to enter except possibly in rare moments of imagina-
> tive daring. We ask ourselves if what we have to meet there
> is not a kind of speculation that lacks any connection with
> our world. Worse, are we perhaps entering that twilight
> realm which deduces our generation away from meeting its
> tasks in the here and now?[1]

Because of its strangeness, the first Jesuit scholars who encountered

with Chinese civilization denounced it as insane and heretic. In spite of the apparent difficulties in connecting the I Ching with the Western

mind of our time, as we have already pointed out, there are amazing

similarities between them.

The cosmology, the structural aspects of cosmic process, that the

I Ching presupposes is far more relevant than that of the classical science

to the understanding of modern science. Thus Wilfred C. Smith says,

"Some observers hold that twentieth-century science in the West is

moving closer to a fundamental yin-yang type of interpretation of the

natural universe than traditional Western views."[2] The traditional

Western view of the world or the classical scientific cosmology is

characterized with materialistic, mechanistic and deterministic outlooks.

In this kind of world view things are thought to move in time and space

according to the definite order. Space and time are regarded as indepen-

dent realities. This idea is clearly expressed in the three-dimensional

space of Euclidian geometry. Since time is an independent reality, it

occupies an absolute category which is a priori to all other existence.

The Euclidian concept of time and space as absolute categories had pre-

vailed until the beginning of the twentieth-century. Even Newtonian

physics did not make any radical break with this kind of static cosmology.

For him time and space are absolute and a priori categories to all other

existence. Within the fixed space and time events are understood to be

governed by the strict law of causality, which is the basis of the

deterministic view of the world. Since everything operates according to
the cause and effect principle, the future phenomena are predictable.
The world is similar to a machine which follows the law of cause and
effect. This kind of world view is certainly strange to the world view of
the I Ching. However, the world view that classical science has held
for many centuries is altered by development of modern science in the
twentieth-century. The new world view, which is primarily attributed to
Albert Einstein, is, as we said, amazingly similar to the cosmology of
the I Ching.

The world view which is based on the theory of relativity and
quantum mechanics is similar to the organic view of the world, which the
I Ching suggests. Unlike the mechanistic world view, the organic view
of the world denies any absolute space and time categorization. In it
time and space are no longer a priori categories for other existence, but
are mutually interdependent. Time as well as space become the dimensions of existence. In this world of interdependence nothing is isolated
from the whole. Everything is related to everything else as if it were
part of one organism. This kind of organic view of the world was already
latent in the idea of Darwin, Freud and Einstein, who got away from the
mechanistic view of the traditional world. The tendency of contemporary
science to get away from the mechanistic materialism was strongly stimu-
lated, if not indeed derived from, the organic world-outlook which is

characteristically Chinese.[3] As we have already indicated, the basic

principle of changing process in the I Ching presupposes the organic

view of the world. In other words, change is always accompanied with

procreativity, which is the essential quality of any organism. Just as the

interaction of yin and yang presupposes their offspring, the concept of

change in the I Ching presupposes creative process. This kind of world

view became important in a later period to the development of Neo-

Confucian organic naturalism by many scholars such as Chuang Chou,

Chou Tun-i, Chu Hsi and many others. Needham seems to summarize

the importance of organic view of Chinese philosophy to the development

of contemporary science. He says,

> . . . the time was to come when the growth of knowledge
> necessitated the adoption of a more organic philosophy no
> less naturalistic than atomic materialism. That was the
> time of Darwin, Frazer, Pasteur, Freud, Spemann, Planck,
> and Einstein. When it came, a line of philosophical
> thinkers was found to have prepared the way--from
> Whitehead back to Engels and Hegel, from Hegel to
> Leibniz--and then perhaps the inspiration was not
> European at all. Perhaps the theoretical foundations of
> the most modern 'European' natural science owe more to
> men such as Chuang Chou, Chou Tun-I and Chu Hsi than
> the world has yet realized.[4]

Since the rise of the organic philosophy of Neo-Confucianism was largely

based on the cosmology of the I Ching, especially on Chou Tun-i's dis-

covery of the T'ai Chi T'u (太極圖) or the Diagram of the Supreme

Ultimate, the I Ching can be regarded as the foundation of the most modern view of the world.[5]

The organic view of the world, unlike the materialistic view of it, is then based on the idea that the world is constantly in the process of change and transformation. The world changes, because, according to the I Ching, the essence of the world is none other than change itself. Everything is in the process of becoming because of the Change which changes all things. The dynamic process of change and transformation is clearly expressed within the study of astronomic science as well as the study of quantum mechanics. "The galaxies recede from one another, and new ones are formed by condensation out of the newly created matter, which takes the place of the old ones which have moved away."[6] The old galaxies disappear and the new ones are formed. In the microcosmic level there seems to exist a similar pattern of process. The ever-moving orbital electrons and nucleus in the sub-atomic structure seem to confirm the world of constant change and transformation. The world is then similar to an ever-flowing river, the flux, which is relative. The world is relative because it is constantly changing.

Einstein's theory of relativity presupposes the changing world. It denies that the world is static and absolute. Time and space are not independent. They are mutually complementary to each other. Time is no longer a priori category by which measurements are inferred. "The theory of relativity acknowledges that frames of reference are relative, and that one is as good as another."[7] All motion is relative. "In general, we cannot say that an object has a velocity of such-and-such, but must say that it has a velocity of such-and-such relative to so-and-so."[8] In the world of relativity we cannot speak anything objectively without making reference to its relationship with others. For example, the movement of a car at fifty miles an hour must be understood in relation to the movement of earth. It is then the relationship or the relatedness which provides meaning. In other words, we can speak things meaningfully because of their relationship. This idea is central to the yin and yang relationship in the I Ching. As we have indicated, yin and yang are descriptive symbols of relationship. They are always relative to each other. Yin is always relative to yang, and yang is relative to yin in all circumstances. Yin loses its meaning when its relationship with yang is lost. Yang is also yang because of yin. Their existence is conditioned by relationship. Thus yin is meaningful only in its relation to yang, just as yang finds its meaning when it is related to yin. The basic principle which underlies the theory of relativity is then implicit in the symbols of yin and yang in the I Ching.

The significance of the yin-yang relationship is clearly expressed in Einstein's special theory of relativity, which we have already used to explain the relativity of mass and energy relationship. For a detailed examination, let us take up this theory which is summarized with the

mass-energy equivalence formula, $E = mc^2$. Here, E signifies energy

that is contained in a stationary body, and m is its mass. C represents

the velocity of light, about 186,000 miles per second. This formula

simply explains that the energy that belongs to the mass is equal to this

mass, multiplied by the squares of the enormous speed of light. This

means that a vast amount of energy is needed for every unit of mass.

However, what is important in this formula is the interdependence between

energy and mass. Since c^2 represents constance, it is a conditional

factor. In other words, when the condition of c^2 is provided, mass can

become energy and energy become mass. They are interchangeable when

the condition c^2 is provided. Therefore, E or energy is always relative

to mass m, just as mass is relative to energy. The formula provides the

relative of energy to mass and that of mass to energy. In this respect,

energy cannot exist without mass, just as mass cannot exist without

energy. They are, then, practically identical with the yin and yang

relationship. Just as yin is relative to yang and yang to yin, mass is

relative to energy and energy to mass. The interdependency of counter-

parts is then an indispensable aspect of the relativity theory. Since one

is inseparable from the other, it is not possible to describe one without

its relation to the other. It is, in other words, the denial of any absolute which is totally independent from others. Thus the world that the theory

of relativity presupposes is more organic than mechanical in nature.

The theory of relativity denies not only the absolute category of

description but also the deterministic view of the world. Determinism

has been held seriously in the mechanical view of the world. However,

in the organic and relativistic view of the world determinism is no longer

real. Thus Max Born denounces material determinism. He says:

> An unrestricted belief in causality leads necessarily to the
> idea that the world is an automation of which we ourselves
> are only little cogwheels. This means materialistic deter-
> minism. It resembles very much that religious determinism
> accepted by different creeds, where the actions of men are
> believed to be determined from the beginning by a ruling of
> God. I cannot enlarge on the difficulties of which this idea
> leads if considered from the standpoint of ethical responsi-
> bility. The notion of divine predestination clashes with the
> notion of free will, in the same way as the assumption of an
> endless chain of natural causes.[9]

The mechanical view of the world is deterministic, because it is based on

the causality principle. This kind of deterministic world is not compatible

with the living organism. In the organic view of the world where every-

thing is interdependent chance plays an important role. The random

principle or chance, rather than the deterministic principle, seems to

work in the biological science. Thus, "Darwinism in its present form--

chance mutation and selection--cannot possibly account for all the

different organic forms we find on earth."[10] However, the practical

importance of the causality principle in our common situation cannot be

denied. For example, "In the solar system we can predict fairly accurately how many eclipses of the sun will happen in a thousand years--
predict fairly accurately the date and time of each particular eclipse."[11]
Nevertheless, the causality principle seems to fail when it deals with the
sub-atomic phenomena. As Eddington indicates, "Anything which depends
on the relative location of electrons in an atom is unpredictable more than
a minute fraction of a second ahead."[12] This is then the famous Principle
of Indeterminacy or the Principle of Uncertainty by Werner Heisenberg.
However, not all physicists have welcomed indeterminism. Einstein himself found it unacceptable. "God does not throw dice" was the well-
known phrase of Einstein's challenge to the idea of indeterminism, to
which Niels Bohr replied: "Nor is it our business to prescribe to God how
He should run the world."[13] However, the majority of quantum theorists
in our time seem to have accepted the Principle of Indeterminacy. Thus,
Koestler says, "Heisenberg will probably go down in history as the man
who put an end to causal determinism in physics--and thereby in
philosophy--with his celebrated Principle of Indeterminacy for which he
got the Nobel Prize in 1931."[14] The Principle of Indeterminacy, which
Heisenberg coined,[15] is directly connected with the relativistic view of
the world. In the sub-atomic situation, as Heisenberg suggests, "we
cannot make observations without disturbing the phenomena--the quantum
effects we introduce with our observation automatically introduce a degree

of uncertainty into the phenomenon to be observed. This Einstein refused to accept, although he knows the facts perfectly well."[16] According to the Indeterministic Principle, the more precisely the location of an electron is determined, for example, the more uncertain its velocity becomes; and vice versa. This kind of paradox is certainly akin to the basic philosophy of the I Ching and Taoistic tradition. Lao Tzu expresses it in a different way: "Those who speak do not know; those who know do not speak." When we say "this is it," it is no longer it. The more precisely we describe the Tao, the more absurd it becomes to us. This paradox makes sense if we look at the Tao in terms of yin and yang relationship. Since "one yin and one yang are called the Tao,"[17] to know the Tao is to know the relationship between yin and yang together. Yin and yang are primarily relational, and indeterminancy results when the relational aspect is not considered. For example, when we observe yin alone without its relationship with yang, yang is not apprehended. The same kind of relationship is also inherent in yang. When yang alone is objectified, yin becomes absurd. If we focus to one, the other becomes blurred. If yin grows, yang decays. If yang becomes clear, yin becomes obscured. They are mutually relative but also reversely proportioned in all respect. When one increases, the other decreases. This kind of mutually complementary relationship makes the idea of indeterminancy possible. Therefore, there is no way to objectify the phenomenon as we have done in classical science. As Heisenberg suggests, "It simply means that we cannot objectify the observational results in the manner of classical physics or everyday experience. Different observational situations--by that I mean the overall experimental step, the readings, etc.--are often complementary, i.e., they are mutually exclusive, cannot be obtained simultaneously and their result cannot be correlated without further ado."[18] Just as yin and yang are mutually exclusive and complementary, their relationship is more paradoxical than rational and causal in our experience. The idea of indeterminancy takes an important role in the divination process of the I Ching. The divination process through the use of stalks or coins is based purely on chance, because the yin and yang relationship is inherently indeterministic. Carl Jung has coined the term synchronicity or an acausal connecting principle to describe this chance operation, which is "the simultaneous occurrence of two meaningfully but not causally connected events."[19] Jung attempts to give meaning to chance through the acausal connecting principle. Even though the principle of indeterminacy and the acausal connecting principle are not identical, both of them attempt to find meaning in the non-causal phenomena. The former is more relevant to quantum mechanics, while the latter to psychic conditions.

One of the most interesting phenomena which both the I Ching and modern science share together is the complementarity of opposites.

According to the I Ching everything consists of yin and yang, which are the basic constituents of all things. In other words, when there is yin, there must be yang. One does not exist without its counterpart. This idea seems to be realized in quantum mechanics as well. One of the most important discoveries that Paul Adrian Maurice Dirac of Cambridge made deals with anti-electrons. This discovery began with his study of space as the limitless sea of electrons or negative energy. However, later he found a "hole" or bubble in the sea of negatively charged electrons. This hole is known as the negation of an electron; therefore, it has a positive charge. Since the discovery of the anti-electron, many other anti-particles have been discovered. More than fifty particles in our day are known as "antis." They seem to have opposite electric charges, magnetic moments and opposite spin. The discovery of counterparts is certainly an important event, which strangely coincides with yin and yang. Thus, Heisenberg says, "Thanks to Dirac's discovery, i.e., the existence of antimatter."[20] Even though it is difficult to generalize our application of the relationship between matter and antimatter in metaphysical considerations, it seems to suggest the coexistence of counterparts which is very fundamental to the relationship of yin and yang. When there is positive, there is also negative. When there is strong, there must be weak. When there is good, there must be evil. Just as yin presupposes the existence of yang and yang that of yin, matter seems to presuppose the existence of its counterpart, the antimatter.

Even though these counterparts are exclusive because of their opposite character, they are complementary to each other. Yin and yang are opposite. They are exclusive in this sense. However, their exclusiveness is relative to their unity. In other words, their diversity is found within their unity. This idea is so closely associated with the Diagram of the Great Ultimate, where yin and yang are intertwined. However, yin is dark, and yang is bright. Yin is negative, while yang is positive. Yin is passive and yang is active, and so forth. Since their exclusive characters are subordinated to the wholeness to which they belong, they do not conflict but complement each other. We see quite a similar phenomenon in quantum mechanics. This is known by the Principle of Complementarity discovered by the great Danish physicist Niels Bohr. Bohr's discovery of this principle is based on the recognition that the light behaves as both a wave and corpuscle. Heisenberg, one of his close associates, remarks: "After the discovery of the quantum of action by Planck the first and most important step was the recognition (achieved by Lenard's investigations and their interpretation by Einstein) that light, in spite of its wave nature as shown by countless experiments of interference, nevertheless does show corpuscular properties in certain experiments."[21] It involves the inner contraction from the point of view of classical science. However, "The electron," as de Broglie said, "is at once a corpuscle and a wave."[22] It is then the simultaneous coexistence of opposites. This means then the light as wavelike is also the light as a corpuscle at the same time. This kind of relationship is so fundamental to the yin and yang relationship in the I Ching that anyone who knows the basic philosophy of the I Ching does not have any difficulty grasping it. Heisenberg seems to point out the Chinese philosophers of the I Ching when he said: "The concept of complementarity, for instance, which Niels Bohr considers so crucial in the interpretation of quantum theory, was by no means unknown to philosophers, even if they did not express it so succinctly."[23] This idea is different from the Cartesian dualism of matter and mind. It does not belong to the absolute dualism of Cartesianism but to the relative dualism, that is, dualistic frame of reference is relative to the single reality. Heisenberg explains Bohr's concept of complementarity as a way "to describe a situation in which it is possible to grasp one and the same event by two distinct modes of interpretation. These two modes are mutually exclusive, but they also complement each other, and it is only through their juxtaposition that the perceptual content of a phenomenon is fully brought out."[24] What Heisenberg attempts to say here is almost explicitly said by the I Ching, which attempts to explain the changing process by the interaction of yin and yang counterparts. Yin and yang are mutually exclusive but are complementary in the process of change and transformation. It seems though that the basic structure of the microcosmic world is known more in the complementarity of opposites than in the like-with-like relationship. In an autobiographical account Watson describes that the discovery of the structure of DNA was due to thinking along the line of complementarity of opposites rather than following the traditional thinking dealing with the like-with-like idea.[25] The I Ching which attempts to describe everything in terms of the complementarity of opposites certainly concurs with the recent development of modern science.

When we come to the structural aspects of particles, we also see somewhat similarities between quantum mechanics and the I Ching. Even though it is not possible to make real comparison between them, some of the basic hypotheses are similar. First of all, the atomic nucleus and hexagrams are analogous. Both of them are microcosms of the universe. Hexagrams are known as the germinal situations of the universe. They are analogous with seeds which contain all the potential possibilities of everything in the world. Thus it is said, "For he knows the seeds, which are the slight beginnings of movement and the initial indications of good fortune and misfortune. The superior man sees the seeds [hexagrams] and acts immediately without a delay of a single day."[26] These seeds or hexagrams are analogous with the structures of atomic nucleus, which are also the germinal patterns which contain all the potential becomings.

Both hexagrams and atomic nucleons are similar in their constituents. Hexagrams which are combinations of two trigrams can be reduced to two different properties: yin and yang lines or the broken and the unbroken lines. Hexagrams differ from each other because of different combinations of yin and yang lines. A similar phenomenon is also found in the atomic nucleons, which also consist of protons and neutrons. Even though they are different, they can be reduced to two basic factors: positive and negative electronic states. In other words, "protons and neutrons are now considered simply as two different electronic states of the same elementary heavy article known as the 'nucleion.'"[27] To say it in another way, proton is nothing but a charged neutron, and the neutron is nothing but an uncharged proton.[28] The basic constituents of the atomic nucleous are none other than different electronic charges. Moreover, electrons consist of both negative and positive electronic states. As we have indicated, it was Dirac who discovered the positive-electron which is also known as a positron. Therefore, the atomic structure is governed by positive and negative electronic forces, just as the hexagram is ruled by the yin and yang lines. We also see the similarity in the process of their structural changes from one form to the other. When one line of the hexagram changes from yin to yang or from yang to yin, the new hexagram is formed. For example, let us observe the change of the hexagram 2, K'un (坤) to the hexagram 24, Fu (復). As we notice from the diagrams, when the first line (always count from below) of K'un changes

from yin or the divided line to yang or the undivided line, the situation

```
 ___ ___          ___ ___
 ___ ___          ___ ___
 ___ ___          ___ ___
 ___ ___          ___ ___
 ___ ___          ___ ___
 ___ ___          _____

  K'un              Fu
```

changes. K'un is the symbol of receptivity or earth, while Fu is the

symbol of returning. Here, we see that the change of one line brings

forth a new situation in the I Ching. In the structure of atomic nucleus

there seems to take a similar pattern of changes. When the delicate

balance between neutron and proton, which is maintained by the activity

of pion, is upset, it is believed that the new atomic structure or the new

situation is to be formed. In both cases the change of new structure

takes place when they cannot maintain the delicacy of their structural

balance. The failure to maintain the structural balance is due to the

redundancy of positive or negative charges. In the hexagram we notice

the change of yin to yang or yang to yin is based on the redundancy which

seems to upset the balance of structure. The delicate balance of atomic

structure cannot be also maintained when the redundancy of either positive

or negative electronic state occurs. In the I Ching we see clearly how the redundancy of either yin or yang or negative or positive will alter the line, which in turn changes the hexagram. As we have indicated, duograms indicate the process of change from one line to the other. The combination of two lines makes duograms possible. At young yin (☷) the balance of yin and yang or divided and undivided line is maintained. Thus it is in a steady state. However, when it changes to old yin (☷) the balance is upset because of the excess or redundancy of yin. Thus it changes to young yang (☳). Again when yang or the undivided line exceeds its growth, it becomes the old yang (☰), which then changes to young yin again. As we notice from the patterns of changing process, the redundancy of either positive or negative upsets the balance of germinal structure. Since the change of line is responsible for the change of hexagrams, all the changes of the world can be reduced to the change of yin to yang or yang to yin. The way of change from one state to another is then simple. The change of yin to yang or yang to yin is due to the union and separation of line. Yin or the divided line (— —) becomes yang or the undivided line (———) by union. Closing and opening changes lines from one state to another. It is then analogous with the emission and addition of electron to change the structure of atomic nucleus. This phenomenon is far more interesting if we consider the value numbers of yin and yang together. Yin has the value number two, and yang the value number three.[29] When yin or negative changes to yang or positive, the

value number one is added to it. When yang or positive changes to yin
or negative, the value number one is omitted. Therefore, the change of
positive to negative or negative to positive, that is the change of yang
to yin or yin to yang, is due to the addition or omission of one or quantum.
As a result we see much similarity between the structural nature of
atomic nucleos and hexagrams.

The I Ching is also relevant to the development of the computer
science in our time. The most used number system in computer science
is the binary system, which is inherent in the very structure of hexagrams. The binary system is interested in a two-value system, that is,
a closed circuit and an open circuit, "on" and "off," or "Yes" or "No."
The yin and yang lines are almost synonymous to the binary system. The
yin line corresponds to the open circuit, because its shape is open in
the middle (— —). On the other hand, the yang line corresponds to the
closed circuit, because its center is closed (———). The yang line as
positive corresponds to "Yes," and the yin lines as negative correspond
to "No." The former is the "on" position of switches and the latter is
the "off" position. If we substitute the yang line with number one (1)
and the yin line with number zero (0), we begin to see the implications
of hexagrams to the binary system. Let us take up the natural sequence,
which is also known as Fu Hsi's arrangement, of hexagrams and substitute them with 0 and 1 numbers. We will get the following sequence:

000000 (K'un or Earth), 000001 (Pi or Balancing Together), 000010 (Kuan or Contemplation), 000011 (Yu or Enthusiasm), etc. and finally reaches to 111111 (Ch'ien or Heaven). If we observe the diagram which was believed to be arranged by Shao Yung during the Sung dynasty, the circle of the hexagram had to be cut in two, and one-half of it had to be reversed. About 600 years later the chart fell into the hand of Leibniz through one of the Jesuit missionaries in China, Father Joachim Bouvet. This amazing coincidence of Leibniz's binary system and Shao Yung's arrangement of hexagrams has become the real point of interest for the history of science. Was Leibniz's discovery of binary arithmetic independent of Shao Yung's arrangement of hexagrams? Whatever the relationship between Leibniz's work with the natural arrangement of hexa-grams might be, it is reasonable to believe that the usefulness of the binary system was not known until the time of Leibniz. Thus, Martin Gardner is right: "It was not until the time of Leibniz that the Fu Hsi sequence was recognized as being isomorphic with a useful arithmetical notation."[30] Even though the usefulness of the binary system in the I Ching was not known in China, the I Ching had already provided the basic patterns for the development of computer technology in our time. In this respect, Fu Hsi, to whom the natural order of hexagrams is attributed, deserves the credit of appraisal. Thus Leibniz said, "Everybody believes that Fu Hsi was one of the old Emperors of China, one of the best known

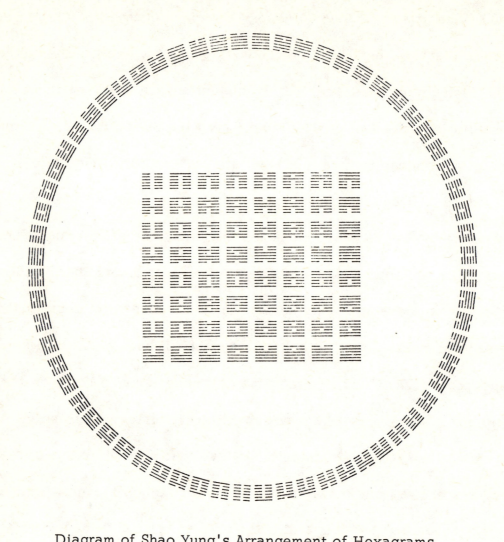

Diagram of Shao Yung's Arrangement of Hexagrams

philosophers of the world, and at the same time the founder of scholarship

in the Chinese Empire and in the Far East. His I Ching table, handed

down to the world, is the oldest monument of scholarship."[31] Since the

I Ching provides the basic patterns for the development of computer

technology, it can be understood as the archetypal computer. What is

fed into this binary system ought to represent all the possible phenomena of the universe. The I Ching is then not only the archetypal but the most archaic computer known in the world. Even though the method of consulting it, that is, the divination process, is so unscientific to us, it has authenticated itself for many centuries in China, Korea and Japan. In this respect Paul Veide is right to call it "poor man's computer."[32]

Finally, the I Ching and modern science are similar, because both of them deal with poetic and symbolic imaginations. Quantum mechanics cannot use a descriptive language in the classical sense. It is best understood as a poetical approach to reality. Thus, in his conversation with Werner Heisenberg, Niels Bohr remarks, "We must be clear that, when it comes to atoms, language can be used only as in poetry. The poet, too, is not nearly so concerned with describing facts as with creating images and establishing mental connections."[33] Language must be poetic, because there is no adequate language to express precisely the nature of sub-atomic phenomena. The I Ching, like the quantum mechanics, never uses descriptive language. It is a poetic and symbolic approach to the reality of a changing universe. Hexagrams are primary symbols, and judgments are written in the form of oracles. Nothing in the I Ching should be interpreted literally. The world of mystery never exhausts itself. It transcends human imagination and intellect. Like the I Ching the frontier of modern science seems to deal with the world of great mystery and wonder. Thus Koestler said, "It is also a world of great mystery and beauty, reflected in those fantastic photographs of events in the bubble-chamber, which show the trajectories of unimaginably small particles, moving at unimaginable speeds in curves and spirals, colliding, recoiling or exploding and giving birth to other particles or wavicles."[34] Both the I Ching and modern science seem to explore the world of mystery which cannot be conveyed with the language of ordinal experience. They can be understood best in poetry.

CHAPTER V

THE I CHING AND ACUPUNCTURE

The word "acupuncture" is no longer foreign to the Western world.
Since President Nixon's China trip, one of the most fascinating phenomena to most Americans has been the use of acupuncture. Dr. Walter
Tkach, the physician to the President, accounts his eye-witness: "I
witnessed only three operations using acupuncture anesthesia, and I'm
writing only about what I actually saw."[1] He was amazed at the efficacy
of acupuncture. According to him, the use of acupuncture seems to be
more effective than the use of conventional anesthetics in America.
Moreover, James Reston, the vice-president of New York Times, became
one of the first Americans who had received acupuncture therapy in
Peking's Anti-Imperialism Hospital, where he was hospitalized for the
removal of his appendix. Since then acupuncture clinics sprouted up
across the country. The use of acupuncture has been seriously suggested
in recent years for both anesthetic and therapeutic purposes.

However, one of the most difficult obstacles in the promotion of
acupuncture clinics in America has been the lack of scientific and
rational basis to explain how and why acupuncture works. In order to

justify the theory of acupuncture there has been much speculation. A

good many American physicians think that the efficacy of acupuncture is

due to autohypnosis. However, this theory fails to explain it, because

total surgical anesthesia by hypnosis does not succeed in more than

approximately 15 to 20 percent of subjects. Moreover, the recent

acupuncture therapy with animals has been successful. Thus it should

be more than autohypnosis. Another attempt to explain the effectiveness

of acupuncture as anesthesia is the method of placebo, a treatment that

the patient believes will be effective. The administration of a placebo

does not affect more than 35 percent of cases. Dr. John Fox believes

that the acupuncture technique is based on the "gate control" theory.

According to this theory, sensations are transmitted through nerve fibers

and must pass through a figurative gate in the spinal cord before they are

transmitted to the brain.[2] Acupuncture enables the gate to be closed so

that painful sensations cannot travel to the brain. This theory seems to

explain the limited use of acupuncture for a minor surgical anesthesia.

However, it cannot explain how acupuncture can cure various symptoms

that the conventional medicine fails to do. The real problem that con-

fronts us in our time is not the factual or empirical evidence to support

the effectiveness of acupuncture but the theoretical framework to explain

its actual workings. For example, there had been a major breakthrough

in scientific research with the publication of an article by Kim Bonghan, a North Korean biologist, who claimed that he had successfully isolated

the vital energy system. According to him, the system is composed of

unobserved corpuscles and ducts through which an acellular yet micro-

scopically observable fluid circles.[3] Even though empirical evidences

are available to support the effectiveness of acupuncture treatment, we

do not have the theoretical or metaphysical frame of reference to explain

how acupuncture works. We need a new approach or a new frame of

reference to support the actual evidence of acupuncture therapy.

Acupuncture originated in the Chinese civilization which is quite differ-

ent from ours. Unless we see it in their civilization from their way of

thinking it is nonsensical and meaningless. "If we use 'scientific

approach to acupuncture' to mean dualistic thinking that separates the

spiritual and the material, then our research will never touch the truth of

acupuncture."[4] Since acupuncture was born in the non-dualistic or

monistic thinking of Chinese civilization which is strongly suggested in

the I Ching, we must begin our understanding of acupuncture from the

study of the Chinese way of thinking which is reflected in their meta-

physical systems.

The theoretical basis of acupuncture lies in the Chinese cosmology,

which is most clearly and strongly suggested in the I Ching. As we have

already pointed out, the I Ching is most of all the book of cosmology in

China. It is perhaps the oldest book which attempts to deal with the structural aspect of the cosmos. The I Ching is, therefore, known as the microcosm of the universe. In the I Ching all natural phenomena are translated into a mathematical language by means of a set of graphic symbols or germinal situations (what Leibniz would have called a "universal character"). Therefore, it is like a dictionary permitting men to read the cosmos like an open book. Because the I Ching is interested in the cosmological system of China, acupuncture is closely related to it. Without knowing the cosmology or metaphysics of the I Ching which deals primarily with the yin and yang relationship, it is almost impossible to understand the underlying philosophy of acupuncture.

Since we have already discussed the cosmology of the I Ching in previous chapters, let us simply summarize its basic characteristics before we examine the theoretical basis of acupuncture. The cosmology of China which is described in the I Ching is first of all monistic or non-dualistic. There is no real conflict between the opposites. White and black, good and evil, or right and wrong are not in conflict but complementary to each other. Everything comes from Tao or Change which is regarded as the ultimate reality, the absolute one. However, one, the symbol of absolute, always manifests itself in terms of two, yin and yang counterparts. Therefore, one is two, just as Change is yin and yang. We may say that one is ideal condition and two in one is actual condition of the ultimate reality. Thus the cosmology of the I Ching is not only interested in the whole but in the harmony of the whole through

the opposites of yin and yang. This principle of harmony between the

opposites becomes the key to the understanding of acupuncture. The use

of acupuncture is none other than to restore the disharmony between the

opposites or yin and yang forces in the body. In other words the function

of acupuncture is to remove any obstacle that prevents the natural flow

of energy which always seeks the harmony and balance of opposites.

The harmony of yin and yang energy is natural and inherent in the structure

of cosmos and man. Thus what acupuncture can do is to remove any

hindrance to the natural course of energy flow. It is then a means to

assist the natural healing or effect natural law. All forms of diseases

are none other than the different manifestations of this single cause,

the imbalance of yin and yang forces, which is the malfunctioning of

natural law of harmony and symmetry. In this respect the theoretical

basis of acupuncture is the concept of Change which operates through the

harmonious interplay of yin and yang.

Another distinctive characteristic of Chinese cosmology which the

I Ching depicts is the micro- and macrocosmic relationship existing in

all things. Man is then the microcosm or the small image of the universe

and is subject to the identical law that governs all things. The universe

is seen as the cosmic person or purusha. The universe is the expansion

of man. Because heaven is round and the earth square, man's head is also round and his foot square. Because heaven has its sun and moon,

man also has eyes and ears. The order of stars is correlated to the set

of teeth. Rain and wind are correlated to man's joy and anger. The

mountains and valleys of earth correspond to man's shoulders and arm-

pits. Rocks and stones are related to nodes and tuberosities. Weeds

and grasses in the field are related to man's hairs and down. Trees and

shrubs parallel man's tendons and muscles. The four seasons of the

year correspond to the four limbs of man. The twelve months are related

to the twelve joints. In this way man is a replica of the universe.

Man's correlation with the universe is clearly expressed in the Chinese

trinity which is symbolized in the trigram. In the trinity man is also

heaven and earth. Lu Hsiang-shan (1139-1193), the founder of the Neo-

Confucianist School of Mind, said, "I lift up my head and grasp at the

Great Dipper. I turned my body round and am in the company of the North

Star. With my head erect I look beyond the Heavens."[5] Because man is

the microcosm of the universe, he can say again: "All the affairs of the

universe come within the range of my duty. My duties include all the

affairs of the universe . . . . The universe is my mind. My mind is

the universe."[6] This idea that man's mind is the microcosm of the

universe seems to be confirmed by the study of contemporary scientists.

Thus Arnold Toynbee said, "We do know, however, that, as a physical

structure, a human brain is comparable to the whole physical universe in movements, and in the complexity of these movements, interrelations.

We also know that there is a correlation between the brain and the psyche

in their respective structures and capacities, each in its own medium."[7]

If the modern view of man confirms the archaic view of the Chinese mind

that man is the microcosm of the universe, it is believable that the

technique of acupuncture which is based on this world view might be

relevant and possibly applicable to the treatment of human diseases.

Since man is a microcosm of the natural world, man's function must

be identical with the function of nature. Just as the I Ching as the

microcosm of the world was based on the observation of natural phenom-

ena, the idea of acupuncture must be based on the observation of the

functions of the natural world. It is said, "The holy sages could observe

all the movements under heaven. They carefully surveyed how these

movements were met and interpenetrated, in order to know the certain

trend of movements."[8] This certain trend of movements is summed up in

yin and yang relationship. The day is governed by light and darkness.

When the light decreases, the darkness increases. When the darkness

decreases, the light increases. The year is governed by the four

seasons. When the winter goes, the spring comes. When spring goes,

the summer comes. When the summer goes, autumn comes. When

autumn goes, the winter comes again. In this way cold and hot are

regulated and circulated in a harmonious manner. In the human body as the microcosm of nature the same pattern of movements takes place. This

trend of movements, that is, the movement toward the harmony of

opposites, is inherent in all things. This trend is possible because of

Change which changes all things. The power of this trend is known as

ch'i (氣), which is a key to the understanding of acupuncture.

The concept of ch'i became important during the Han dynasty for

"Five Elements" school or Wu Hsing Hsue (五 行 學) as well as

during the Sung Dynasty for the Neo-Confucian movement. During the

Han dynasty Tung Chung-shu (董 仲 舒) defines ch'i similar to the

air or ether which is essential for life. He said:

> Within the universe exist the ethers (ch'i 氣) of the yin
> and yang. Men are constantly immersed in them, just as
> fish are constantly immersed in water. The difference
> between them and water is that the turbulence of the latter
> is visible, whereas that of the former is invisible. Man's
> existence in the universe, however, is like a fish's
> attachment to water. Everywhere these ethers are to be
> found, but they are less viscid than water. For water,
> compared with them, is like mud compared with water.
> Thus in the universe there seems to be a nothingness and
> yet there is substance. Men are constantly immersed in
> this eddying mass, with which, whether themselves orderly
> or disorderly, they are carried along in a common current.[9]

Just as the water is essential for fishes to survive, ch'i is also essential

element of living creatures. The universe is a living organism because of

ch'i. Acupuncture makes use of ch'i as the essential element of life.

Thus the use of acupuncture is to restore the free flow of ch'i in the body.

Without ch'i or vital energy man cannot survive. In this respect it is similar to the water for fishes.

In the I-wei Ch'ien-tso-tu (易緯乾鑿度), one of the Han appocrypha on the I Ching, it is indicated that there was first the Great Change or t'ai i (太易), then the Great Beginning or t'ai ch'u (太初), then the Great Origin or t'ai shih (太始), and finally the Great Simplicity or t'ai su (太素). During the time of the Great Change there was no manifestation of ch'i (氣) or vital energy. The Great Beginning was the originator of ch'i; the Great Origin is the originator of forms or hsing (形); the Great Simplicity is the originator of matter or chih (質). In the Great Change, the vital energy (ch'i), forms (hsing) and matter (chih) were undifferentiated.[10] Here, we notice that ch'i is not only the first manifestation of changing process but also the subtlest form of existence. In other words, ch'i or vital energy is neither form nor matter. In the Western tradition we have been accustomed with the coexistence of form and matter, thus it is difficult to conceive of the existence of this third element in the living. Since acupuncture deals with this element or ch'i, it is difficult for the Western mind to comprehend.

The idea of ch'i became the counterpart of li (理) or principle in Neo-Confucianism during the Sung Dynasty. For Chu Hsi (朱熹) the concept of ch'i used to mean the primordial energy which is the source of all becomings. The ultimate reality consists of both li or principle

and ch'i or vitality together. "The ch'i fills the Great Etheral. It goes

up, it comes down, or it flies high without cessation. This is what the

I Ching refers to as the real secret of the Changes . . . . Ch'i, which

sometimes goes up or at other times comes down, is the beginning of

motion or rest. What goes up is the light, yang part, what comes down

is the heavy, yin part."[11] The part of the ch'i which moves is the yang,

while that which remains quiescent is the yin. The ch'i is then not only

the secret of changing process but the continuum of yin and yang forces.

It is best understood as the primordial condition of yin and yang harmony

which is inherent in all things. Because of this inherent harmony of

opposites the ch'i always inclines toward the perfect balance of yin and

yang. When the ch'i is obstructed from its free flow in the body, an

imbalance of yin and yang energy is created. Through acupuncture the

natural flow of ch'i can be restored, so that yin and yang energies are

balanced. Therefore, Chang Tsai (1020-1077) regards the ch'i as the

Great Harmony. Because of this Great Harmony all harmonies of

opposites are possible in the world. Acupuncture works because this

power is actively present in the body.

Since man is a microcosm of the universe, the flow of ch'i in his

body corresponds to the flow of it in the large space of nature. Just as

nature is affected by the seasons, climate and time of day, the ch'i of the human being pulsates according to the rhythm of nature. For example,

in the summer, yang which represents hot is stronger than yin, the cold.

But in the winter yin is stronger than yang. These are normal phenomena

which will not cause illness. However, when yin or yang becomes too

strong or too weak, it is necessary to restore the balance in the body.

This imbalance which causes sickness can be restored through the inser-

tion of needles as prescribed in the <u>Huang-ti Nei-ching</u> (黄帝内經)

or Classic of Internal Medicine of the Yellow Emperor, which has been

regarded as the most authentic book on acupuncture.

According to the Chinese cosmology of <u>yin-yang</u> and of <u>Wu Hsing</u>

schools, the interaction of yin and yang produces the five elements,

which become the bases for all things in the universe. Everything can be

reduced to the five elements, which are again reduced to yin and yang

forces of <u>ch'i</u>. The River Map or <u>Ho T'u</u> (河圖) which became the

basis of the formation of the eight trigrams by Fu Hsi, the legendary king,

consists of the five elements of yin and yang. We have already dis-

cussed the importance of this map in the second chapter; the five elements

are the basis for the construction of trigrams which also represent the

complete units of universe. From the map we see the five elements

represent different directions. Wood is in the direction of East, Fire in

that of the south, metal of the west, water of the north, and earth is at

the center. These five elements also correlate with the elements of the human body. Just as man is the microcosm of the universe, his organs are also replicas of these five elements. Wood corresponds to the liver, fire to the heart, earth to the spleen, metal to the lungs, and water to the kidneys. These are known as ts'ang (臟) or the solid organs, the internal organs which have yin characteristics. Each of the solid organs has a corresponding hollow organ in the body, known as fu (腑). They are the gallbladder which corresponds to the liver, small intestine which corresponds to the heart, stomach corresponding to the spleen, large intestine corresponding to the lungs and bladder corresponding to the kidneys. While ts'ang organs function to store energy or are receptive like yin, fu organs function to activate it or to be creative like yang. Therefore, fu organs are yang in character. Just as yin and yang are mutually interdependent and complementary, the ts'ang and fu organs are mutually correlated in their activities. The imbalance of yin and yang in these organs causes a malfunction of the body. Thus the acupuncturist attempts to restore the harmony of corresponding organs in the treatment of disease.

There are two more organs within the body. They are called the "Triple Warmer" or the "Three Burning Spaces," which are believed to link man and the universe. Another organ is known as the "Gate of Life" or the "Circulation-Sex Organ," which rests between the kidneys. Both of these are unknown in the Western medicine. The Triple Warmer, a yin organ, regulates other organs. It has the three burning spaces: the upper burning space is known to keep food from leaving the stomach, the middle burning space aids digestion, and the lower burning space excretes waste matter. Its main function is then to regulate the process in the body. The Gate of Life is the counterpart of the Triple Warmer and belongs to the yang organ. It produces semen in the male and functions as the uterus in the female. It regulates the generative energy and produces happiness and joy. Both the Triple Warmer and the Gate of Life are indispensable for the balance of yin and yang energy in the body.

With the addition of these two organs we can conclude that acupuncture deals with six yin organs and six yang organs together. The correlation and harmony of these organs makes the balance of yin and yang energy flow possible. The yin organs are then compared with the hexagram K'un, which consists of six yin lines, while the yang organs can be compared with the hexagram Ch'ien which consists of six yang lines. Just as the interaction of K'un or Earth and Ch'ien or Heaven makes all things possible, the correlation of ts'ang organs and fu viscera makes everything function in the body.

Each organ possesses its own channel, which is often called the meridian. It is believed that ch'i energy flows through the meridians that extend into arms and legs beneath the surface of the skin. The meridians are neither the vessels of the circulatory system that carry blood nor are they of the nerve system that is familiar to Western medicine. They are the channels through which the most subtle life energy or ch'i circulates. The basic technique of acupuncture deals with the restoration of the meridians so that the undisrupted flow of ch'i energy can balance the yin and yang forces in the body. Since acupuncture points are located along the meridians, it is almost impossible to treat the patient unless a clear picture of meridians is defined. The twelve channels are the basic and traditionally held meridians. Nowadays acupuncturists seem to use more than fifty different meridians. Also the classical texts used to acknowledge 365 acupuncture points, which are regarded as the basic points. In practice there are more than one thousand points which are connected with the treatment of illness.

The basic channels of ch'i energy are related to the organs. The Gate of Life or the circulation-six meridian runs along the arm from the tip of the middle finger to the chest. The liver meridian extends from the end of the big toe and up into the center of the torso. The Triple Warmer meridian starts at the hand, runs up the shoulder and neck, and ends at the corner of the eye. The gallbladder meridian extends from the middle of the head down along the body to the bottom of the little toe. Since

both the circulation-sex meridian and the liver meridian are yin channels,

they go up from the lower to the upper part of the body. When man raises

both arms and his feet are on the ground, the yin meridians rise from the

feet and the yang meridians descend from the fingers in the air. It is the

yin which occupies the earth and the yang which occupies the heaven.

Thus the gallbladder meridian and the Triple Warmer meridian move down-

ward, for they belong to yang channels. Here, we see that the meridian

of circulation-sex, which is yin, corresponds to the meridian of the Triple

Warmer, which belongs to yang. The meridian of the liver, which is yin,

also corresponds to the meridian of the gallbladder, which is yang. In

this way the correlation of yin and yang meridians is possible. Since

the theory of acupuncture is to balance the yin and yang flow of ch'i in

the body, the balance can be restored without treating directly the organs

or symptoms themselves. The ancient discovery of acupuncture technique

is based on the idea that soldiers wounded by arrows were cured of ail-

ments in other parts of their bodies. Thus the treatment of acupuncture

deals often with the location which seems to bear no relation to the ill-

ness itself. Since illness is treated by restoring the ch'i energy circula-

tion through the meridians rather than the organs themselves, the knowl-

edge of the meridians is so important in the practice of acupuncture.

The rest of the twelve meridians are also correlated in similar ways. The lung meridian begins at the second rib, runs to the shoulder, the arm and to the end of the thumb. The spleen meridian begins at the big toe, moves along the leg, across the front of the body and ends up at the armpit. The small intestine meridian starts with the little finger, extends to the arm, to the neck and ends up at the ear. The bladder meridian begins at the nostrils, goes to the top of the head, then to the neck, the side of the body, then to the leg and finally ends at the big toe. The large intestine meridian starts at the end of the index finger, up to the arm and neck and on to the face, and finally ends up near the corner of the mouth. The stomach meridian starts at the side of the head, runs to the back, to the leg, and ends at the second toe. The heart meridian starts at the top end of the armpit, down to the arm and ends at the little finger. Finally, the kidney meridian starts at the middle of the foot sole, goes up to the leg, through the front of the body, and ends up at the top of the chest between the breasts.[12]

The flow of ch'i in these meridians is reflected in the pulses, which are the chief basis of diagnosis. Since there are twelve major meridians in the body, there are also twelve different pulses. Each of them is associated with a vital organ. The trained acupuncturist can distinguish various pulses, through which he can discover the cause of illness, that

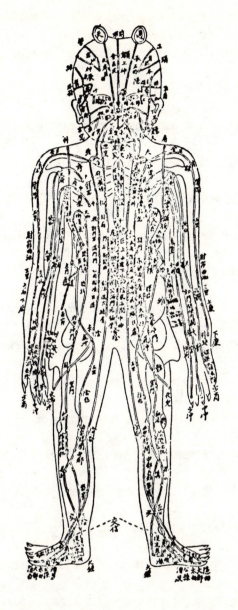

Ancient Acupuncture Chart Showing the Meridians and Points

is, the seat of yin and yang imbalance. It is believed that there are six

different pulses in each arm.

The "superficial" or external pulses differ from the "deep" or the

internal pulses. In each arm there are three external pulses and three internal pulses. Since the internal pulses deal with the internal or yin

organ (ts'ang), they are difficult to detect. On the other hand, the

external pulses which deal with the yang organs or fu are easily notice-

able. On the left wrist there are the inner pulses of heart, liver and

kidney and the external pulses of small intestine, gallbladder and bladder.

On the right wrist there are the inner pulses of lung, spleen and

circulation-sex, and the external pulses of large intestine, stomach and

Triple Warmer. Again the six pulses of each wrist correspond to the six

lines of the hexagram. Just as the hexagram consists of two primary

trigrams--the inner and outer trigrams, the pulses on the wrist consist

of three different inner and outer pulses.

In order to detect the pulses, the acupuncturist will begin with the

left wrist if the patient is a man or the right wrist if the patient is a

woman. Left is characterized by yang, and right by yin. Thus it is

believed that the left wrist of man and the right of woman reveal more

clearly the condition of ch'i circulation. Pulses are also believed to

relate to seasonal changes. The summer pulses, for example, are strong

but fade away quietly. The autumn pulses sound deep and urgent, for the

autumn is characteristic of yin. The acupuncturist often tells the sex of

an unborn baby by pulses. If the unborn baby is a boy, the mother's left

wrist will be rapid and strong, for left signifies yang. If the unborn

baby is a girl, pulses of her right wrist will be rapid and strong.

Moreover, the acupuncturist can detect by pulses the imbalance of yin

and yang before any actual symptom is realized. Therefore, the effective

reading of pulses can be an important contribution to preventive medicine.

There are laws that govern how the treatment of acupuncture is

effected. Since treatment deals with the balance of yin and yang, the

rules are none other than the ways of restoring the balance.

There are four different rules for the acupuncturist to follow. The

acupuncturist can choose any rule that fits a certain circumstance and

symptom. They are the Mother-Son rule, the Husband-Wife rule, the

Noon-Midnight rule and the rule of the Five Elements. They are different

ways to effect the circulation of ch'i in the body, but they are always

interdependent. Since they are mutually inclusive, the acupuncturist

can choose to use more than one rule to treat the patient.

The Mother-Son rule is the direct method of treatment, the direct

influence of one organ on another. By stimulating the mother organ, the

son organ is directly affected. If the ch'i energy begins its cycle from

the lung, it flows through the large intestine, stomach, spleen, heart,

small intestine, bladder, kidneys, circulation-sex, Triple Warmer, gall-

bladder, and liver meridians. If we follow the order of the flow of ch'i

as we have indicated, the lung is the mother organ of the large intestine,

which is its son organ. The large intestine is the mother organ of the

stomach, which is also the son organ of the former. In this way the mother organ directly affects the son organ. By stimulating the mother

organ through acupuncture the son organ is affected for the treatment of

illness. In this treatment the principle of yin-yang relationship is

observed. When the ch'i energy flows from the mother organ to the son,

the former decreases and the latter increases, just as the increase of yin

is the decrease of yang at the same time. It is the direct flow of ch'i in

an inverse proportion. This is then the most simple and direct way to

effect the restoration of the balance of vital energy.

The Husband-Wife rule deals with the horizontal relationship among

the meridians of ch'i flow. Since left is characterized by yang, and right

by yin, the former belongs to husband and the latter to wife. For a man

the left hand meridians are stronger than the right. But for a woman the

right hand meridians are more vital than the left hand. As an acupunctur-

ist knows this rule is important in the treatment of illness and restoring

the balance of vital energy. It is important to see that the meridians

complement each other, just as yin and yang are mutually interdependent.

The Noon-Midnight rule deals with the influence of time on the

flow of ch'i energy. Yang is more active during the daytime, while yin

is more active at night. The former is the principle of light and the latter

of darkness. Yang increases its strength from midnight to noon, while

yin increases its strength from noon to midnight. These two forces are

inversely proportioned. The yin organs respond best in the day, and the yang organs respond best at night. Each organ has its most favorable

hours for acupunctural response. For example, the heart responds best

at noon, while the gallbladder responds best at midnight. Noon is the

best time to stimulate yang, and midnight to activate the yin of ch'i.

The acupuncturist can choose certain times of day to treat the various

symptoms following the rules. Since the human body is the microcosm

of the universe, the change of time and season also affects the change

of the flow of ch'i in the body. The effective treatment of acupuncture

then considers the importance of times and seasons for the treatment of

illness.

Finally, it is important to observe the rule of the Five Elements,

which deals with cosmological implications of acupuncture therapy.

Just as the five essential elements which constitute all things in the uni-

verse are mutually interdependent, the basic organs in the human body

mutually influence each other. When one increases, the other decreases;

when one is strong the other is weak. When yin is too much, yang is too

little. It is the holistic approach to the understanding of the yin-yang

activity in the body. Just as the five elements are mutually dependent,

the ch'i flow of one organ is dependent on other organs. As we have

already pointed out, the five elements are mutually related. Wood pro-

duces fire, fire produces earth, earth metal, metal water, and water

wood. However, fire destroys (or melts) metal, metal destroys wood,

wood again consumes the earth. The earth then destroys (or absorbs)
water, and water destroys fire. They are mutually interdependent. Just
as the relationship among the five elements, the five ta'ang or organs
are mutually interrelated to each other. Any treatment of illness through
acupuncture must observe the rule of the Five Elements.

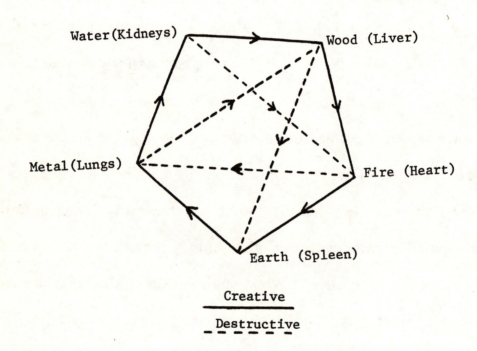

The Rule of the Five Elements

These rules that the acupuncturist must observe in his treatment
of illness are in harmony with the principles of change in the I Ching,
which lays down the basic metaphysical and cosmological principles for

the development of acupuncture techniques in the past. It is, therefore,

difficult to understand the theory of acupuncture without some under-

standing of the I Ching. For those who believe that the I Ching is magic

and occultic, it is. However, for those who see the profundity of the

I Ching, acupuncture is not strange at all. Acupuncture works just as

the I Ching works and has authenticated itself for many milleniums in

China, Korea and Japan.

CHAPTER VI

THE I CHING AND NEW SELF-THERAPY

The I Ching can be easily overlooked for its therapeutic value. It is certainly more than a book of divination, it is also a book of healing. If it is interested only in foretelling the unknown, it is certainly not different from other divination books. The uniqueness of this book seems to lie in its self-therapeutic device. The I Ching not only provides the framework where the healing process of man is realized but becomes a practical instrument that facilitates the actual healing of the whole self. Let us first observe how the I Ching provides such a framework that makes self-therapy possible, before we come to discuss the practical implications toward the self-healing process.

The basic framework which the I Ching provides is most of all a holistic or totalistic view of man and the universe. This holistic approach to reality is fundamental to therapeutic process. Therapy can be understood as the restoration of the broken relationship to the whole. It is the task of integration and renewal. The I Ching provides the holistic framework where the opposites are brought together in harmony with the eternal law of change and transformation. It does not approach man

106

in separation of the universe. It always presents man in his relation to the universe. Man is the microcosm of the universe, and the universe is the macrocosm of man. In this respect the healing of man's illness cannot be treated independently of the universe. As we have already pointed out in the previous chapter, the acupuncture therapy must also consider his relation to the universe. Since man is an integral part of the universe, the health of man presupposes the health of the universe. Thus ecology and therapy are mutually interdependent and complementary. The therapeutic method then not only includes the integration of one's whole self but the integration of oneself with the whole universe. In this regard man cannot be a whole person unless he is a part of the whole universe. If therapy in the past was based on man's individuation without his relation to the universe, the I Ching certainly provides the new therapeutic process of man which involves the total process of the universe. The permanent and sound therapy is possible only when man is in tune with the Tao of the universe. When he is one with it, he is to be restored to his original state and a spontaneous healing takes place. Thus the holistic framework is fundamental to self-therapy.

Just as man's whole self cannot be dealt with without its relation to the total universe, his problem cannot be isolated from the total make-up of his personality. When the problem is dealt with independently of his whole self, it can easily create another problem that distorts the whole system of integration. The therapeutic method can easily fall into the most deadly mistake of treating the symptom without considering the person as a whole. The I Ching attempts to provide a framework where the real therapy deals with the entire person rather than the symptom only. Unless the symptom is considered in relation to the whole person, the real cure is not possible.

The whole person consists of both the male and female or animus and anima. The coexistence of these opposites in man is most clearly expressed in the relationship of yin and yang in the I Ching. Just as yin and yang are mutually interdependent, the animus (or the male in woman) and anima (or the female in man) are mutually inclusive. The whole person is possible through a creative integration of these opposites. This process of integration is known by Jung as the process of individuation.[1] The whole self or the microcosm of the universe is always greater than the sum of yin and yang or anima and animus. Just as the whole is greater than the sum of its parts, the whole person is greater than the mere combination of both the male and female. The goal of therapy is then transformation and renewal through the creative integration of opposites.

It is then the complementary relationship of yin and yang that becomes the foundation of therapy. When yin and yang are in conflict and exclusive, there arise various symptoms in man. The balance of yin and yang is not only essential in physiological therapy but also in psychological treatment of man. A tendency in analytical psychology, particularly in the thought of Carl Jung, is to make use of the male-female archetypes or yin-yang symbols for therapeutic method. Yin and yang or female and male possess exclusive characteristics but are complementary to each other for the reality as a whole. Each individual is both yin and yang or female and male at the same time. Yin is the unifying, dark womb of nature that gives birth to offsprings, yang is the divisive, straight phallus, a sword that penetrates into the depth of all things. Yin is the power of receptivity and yang is the power of creativity. Both of them are completely complementary to each other. Because this complementarity of opposites is inherent in the primordial condition of man, the self-therapy, that is, the restoration of self from conflict to the harmony of opposites, is possible.

The distinction between man and woman is then based on the predominance of yin or yang, that is, anima or animus. Man is characterized by the predominance of manifest yang and of a recessiveness or background functioning of yin. On the other hand, woman is characterized by the predominance of yin and the recessiveness or background functioning of yang.[2] The recessive or background element is latent and, therefore, it is unconscious. On the other hand, the apparent or foreground element is conscious. However, the manifest characteristics need not necessarily be fully conscious either. "Man may be partly unaware of his full masculinity and a woman unaware of the full range of her femininity."[3] This typological classification of man and woman or yang and yin personality is analogous, for example, with the first and second hexagrams in the I Ching. The first hexagram, Ch'ien or creative element, which is characterized with a perfectly manifest yang, presupposes the existence of its background, the second hexagram, K'un or receptive element. The latter also presupposes its background, the former. Just as yin presupposes yang and yang presupposes yin, the predominance of yang presupposes the recessiveness of yin, and the predominance of yin presupposes the recessiveness of yang.

Since predominance is characterized by the conscious element and the recessive element by the unconscious, psychotherapy deals primarily with the creative integration of the conscious and unconscious in man. It is the synthesis that makes the individuation possible. In this creative integration the unconscious is brought into the process of conscious realization. In other words, the key to psychotherapy is conscious of the unconscious.[4] This does not mean to transform the unconscious to the conscious realm. Rather it means to be aware of the unconscious as the background of conscious activity. It is not the compromise between the urges of the unconscious id and conscious demands of the superego. Therapeutic method must be understood as the creative harmony between these two forces in man. From Freud's point of view the unconscious is

essentially the seat of irrationality and blind impulse which must be

overcome by the conscious power. In this respect the key to Freudian

psychotherapy is to transform the unconscious to the conscious. How-

ever, in Jung's view, the meaning seems to be reversed; the unconscious

is essentially the seat of the deepest sources of wisdom, while the

conscious is the superficial part of the whole personality.[5] The I Ching

seems to go along with Jung's view that the unconscious is the other side

of the conscious and the source of the latter. Therapy deals with the

harmonious coexistence of both rather than the elimination of one for the

sake of the other.

> For Jung the conscious and unconscious are part of man.
> They have a correlating function so that in the beginning
> the unconscious plays the role of compensating power, of
> a natural complement to the conscious. If this role
> becomes impossible the unconscious takes on the role of
> the opposition, of the adversary.[6]

It is then a mistake to replace the unconscious with the conscious or id

with Ego, if we believe that both of them are complementary for the whole

man. Just as yin is not possible without yang in it and yang is not

possible without yin in it, the conscious cannot be separated from the

unconscious just as the unconscious cannot be conceived without the

unconscious. Thus Jung writes: "Thus we arrive at the paradoxical con-

clusion that there is no content of consciousness which in another respect would not be unconscious. Perhaps there is also no unconscious psychic content which is not at the same time conscious."[7] Because of this complementary relationship the therapeutic method should be the correlation of the conscious and the unconscious rather than the transformation of one into the other.

The creative union of the conscious and the unconscious in the process of self-realization is possible through the images of experience which are known as symbols.

> The symbol is the expression of a union of psychic opposites (Sym-ballein); what other-wise remains separate is, in the symbol, combined into a more complete wholeness and unity; instinct and spirit, feminine and masculine, knowledge and faith, temporal and supratemporal, finite and infinite.[8]

In the symbol man's consciousness is related to the unconscious. It has the power of unity and integration of opposites, because it is the objectification of the inner and spiritual reality which are unconscious in the conscious mind. Symbols are more than representational forms which serve our cognitive process. They are highly potent powers which point beyond the visible and conscious objects. These potent symbols are most clearly expressed in the 64 hexagrams in the I Ching. As we have already pointed out the 64 hexagrams are none other than the all possible combinations of eight trigrams, which are the most fundamental symbols of everything that exists in the universe. These primoridal symbols serve not only the expression of a greater wholeness but the expression of dynmatic forces that urges toward the realization of wholeness and unity

between opposites. Because symbols convey the power beyond them-

selves, therapy becomes a symbolic quest.

If the function of therapy is none other than the symbolic quest, the

I Ching which is the symbolic expression of hexagrams should provide the

background of therapeutic functions. First of all the hexagram suggests

the symbolic union of the conscious and the unconscious. Since the

hexagram consists of two trigrams, it can be considered to be the union

of both the conscious and the unconscious. The inner trigram represents

the unconscious realm, while the outer trigram symbolizes the conscious.

Let us take the last hexagram, Wei Chi (未濟) or Before Completion.

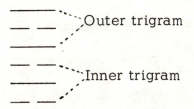

As we see the inner trigram (☵) is K'an (坎) which is known as the

symbol of water, and the outer trigram (☲) is Li (離) or the symbol

of fire. The inner trigram which is symbolized by water represents the

unconscious, and the outer trigram which is symbolized by fire represents

the conscious. The hexagram Wei Chi is the union of these two. Thus it

has the unifying power of opposites. It brings them into harmonious

coexistence. Thus the symbol of this hexagram means: "Fire over water,"
which is characterized in the I Ching as the condition of incomplete.
What we see from the symbol of the hexagram is the very nature of symbol
itself, that is, the union of opposites (sym-ballein). All the 64 hexagrams
in the I Ching can be understood as the union of psychic opposites, the
union of the unconscious (the inner trigram) and the conscious (the outer
trigram).

Hexagrams in the I Ching are known as the primordial images which
are also known as archetypes. According to Carl Jung, the idea of
archetypes was already known in Plato's notion of form (eidola). Moreover, the idea was well known in the teachings of Augustine, who spoke
of "principle" ideas which were not formed but eternally existing in the
divine understanding. These principle ideas or typical images are known
as archetypes.[9] The archetypes are eternally inherited forms without any
specific contents. Since these images are thought of as without content,
they are unconscious. They can attain a content or consciousness by
encountering empirical facts which touch and awaken the unconscious
form.[10] These primordial and principle images, which are organs of the
pre-rational psyche, are manifest in visions, dreams or fantasy. According to legend, King Wen, the author of 64 hexagrams in the I Ching, saw
on a prison wall the visions of various symbols. They later became the
symbols of hexagrams in the I Ching. Just as the hexagrams were

manifested in the vision of King Wen, the archetypes often appear as the visions of mandala, images, figures with specific contents. They commonly manifest themselves in dreams. Thus the analysis of dreams becomes an important part of psychotherapy. Even though the archetypes were given different contents in different situations, they are universal. "They are directly related to the deepest ground of human striving. They are Being and Vision at one and the same time."[11] They are the bases for meaning and ground of human existence. "They correspond to the truths of life."[12] The fundamental principle of therapy is then the actualization of archetypes in life. In the primitive tradition the realization of archetypes was enacted through the religious ceremonies and rites. Priests in this respect took the role of psychotherapists. The chief function of therapists certainly deals with the interpretation of these symbolic manifestations in dreams, hallucinations or other forms of visionary appearances, so that they can be meaningfully integrated into the actual and concrete life situations. The archetypes must be brought to light and translated into the language of consciousness that we can explain through our rational and empirical means. The I Ching not only provides the archetypical symbols through hexagrams but also the actual interpretations of these symbols in the language of consciousness. Therefore, the I Ching is an already-made book of therapy and does not necessitate a middleman or a professional psychoanalyst. In this respect the I Ching is a book for self-therapy.

Let us now focus our attention to the practical implications of the I Ching for the actual process of self-therapy. Since the I Ching has been known primarily as the book of divination, it is better to begin our understanding of its therapeutic value in the actual practice of divination. The entire process of divination in the I Ching has definite implications to the realization of self-therapy. Let us examine how the divination and therapeutic processes are mutually intertwined in the I Ching.

The actual divination process begins with the formulation of questions. Unless the question is defined clearly, the questioner cannot expect to get a definite answer. What is most important in this initial stage is not the definition of the problem itself but the actual process of defining it. In other words, in a therapeutic process it is our struggle and attempt to understand the nature of our symptom in relation to the whole person. It is to be understood as the process of describing the symptom that we know by ourselves. The process of formulating the question for divination is then analagous with the clear understanding of our symptom. Accurate descriptions are almost essential for the correct understanding of our symptom. We have to make accurate descriptions about our illness so that the doctor makes a correct diagnosis. Likewise, we have to know all the facts about our problem before we get to know the problem itself. In this process of self-description we can concentrate our attention on the actual symptom itself. When the problem is clearly defined, we must go through the actual process of divination through the use of yarrow stalks or coins.

The actual process of dividing the yarrow stalks or tossing coins is self-therapeutic in itself. It is the most solemn moment of the therapeutic process. It can be compared with the actual enactment of ritualistic process by which the archetype is disclosed to the language of our consciousness. In other words, it is the process of ritualistic perfection and meditative realization that detaches us from the superficiality of our lives that creates all the problems and illnesses. From many experiences of conducting the divination process in classroom situations in the past, I have come to notice that the most meaningful thing that has happened to students was the actual performance of dividing the yarrow stalks. The process is correlated with the cosmic structure of the universe and seasons of the year.[13] In this process we become one with the cosmos and lose our separate existences. It is the separate identity of ourselves that creates many emotional and psychological problems in our time. Our concentration on the actual performance frees us from the separate self and unites us with the whole. In this unity we are restored to whole personhood. Thus the actual process of dividing yarrow stalks itself has a profound therapeutic value.

Through the process of dividing the yarrow stalks the hexagram is selected. If there is a moving line or lines in the original hexagram which we obtained through the division of yarrow stalks or tossing the coins, there comes another hexagram which is known as the consequent hexagram. The former is known in Chinese as the yuan kua (原卦), which depicts the actual situation of the symptom itself, and the latter is known as the chih kua (之卦), which attempt to show the future realization of the original situation. Let us suppose that the original hexagram we received through the process of dividing the yarrow stalks was the 23rd hexagram, Po (剝) or Peeling, which consists of five yin lines and one yang line on the top. If the first line is the moving

```
———————        ———————
——  ——         ——  ——
——  ——         ——  ——
——  ——         ——  ——
——  ——         ——  ——
——  ——         ———————

   Po              I
```

line, the consequent hexagram is the 27th, I (頤) or Cheek, which consists of two yang lines on the first and last places and four yin lines between them. They are archetypical forms which are universal in character. These hexagrams are without content as are the archetypes. Thus they are unconscious by themselves. These archetypical forms are waiting our response, so that they can be brought to light and translated into the language of our consciousness. Thus Carl Jung said, "The Chinese sage would smilingly tell me: 'Don't you see how useful the I Ching is in making you project your hitherto unrealized thoughts into its abstruse symbolism?'"[14] These archetypes wait for us to fill with the experience which is latent and not easily available to our conscious lives. In other words, the hexagrams can serve the most meaningful vehicles for us or project the subconscious experience that is not available by any other means. They are far more effective means than the ink-blot designs being used by the Rorscharch test. The ink-blot designs are not the eternally inherent forms or archetypes, while the hexagrams are. The latter can provide a certain framework which is universal to all other experiences. In this respect the hexagrams as archetypes are far more meaningful symbols than ink-blot designs for the projection of our latent experience. In other words, the hexagrams are more suggestive than the ink-blot designs. The absurdity of symbolism can provide considerable latitude in interpretation. Let us attempt to demonstrate how effective the hexagrams are to understand our hidden experience which is not conscious in life.

Suppose we have a problem that annoys us. After a careful con-
sideration and definition of the problem by ourselves, we may decide to
consult the I Ching to understand the problem and to solve it by ourselves.
Through a careful and mediative process of manipulating the stalks we
have obtained the hexagram which should correspond to the question we
have asked. Suppose the hexagram which we have obtained is the 25th,
Wu Wang (无 妄) or Innocence, which consists of Chen or thunder

```
━━━━━━
━━━━━━
━━  ━━
━━  ━━
━━━━━━
```

(☳) and Ch'ien or heaven (☰). We must concentrate on the
hexagram and try to bring out all the possible implications of this symbol
to our condition. We have to carry it with us as our own mandala to
solve the problem by ourselves. As we contemplate and reflect upon
the hexagram, we may be able to project subconscious feelings that are
relevant to the understanding of the underlying problem. It is possible
that we may think of the thunder that shakes heaven, since the hexagram
consists of the images of heaven and thunder. It seems to suggest that
the cause of the real problem lies in our earliest experience of seeing the
terrible power of thunder that strikes heaven. In any case the hexagram

can serve as a means by which our unconscious feelings and experiences
are projected and brought into the realm of consciousness. If the real
cause of our trouble has to do with the childhood experience of thunder
and lightning that shook the heaven, the problem is based on the
innocence of our childhood. It is not based on willful wrong behavior or
sinful act. The fear based on a child's naivete is certainly innocent.
Thus the judgment on this hexagram says: "Wu Wang (Innocence) has
supreme success. Faithfulness to our own self will be advantageous.
If we are not as we should be, we cannot succeed in any thing." The
judgment is an interpretation of the hexagram in the language of consciousness. Since the symbol is already interpreted in the I Ching, it
is not necessary to have the professional therapist analyze the symbol.
However, the judgment is not descriptive. It can be compared to the
parable or poem which needs our personal interpretation. The judgment
should be also the object of our contemplation and careful reflection, so
that our unconscious feelings are fully revealed to the frame of our conscious reference. In this way the diagnostic process can take place
without any assistance of a professional therapist.

The I Ching also provides a prescription. It tells us what to do to
remedy the problem. The prescription is described in the judgment. As
in the case of the hexagram on Innocence, the prescription is to be faith-
ful to our own nature for success. The problem is due to the

unfaithfulness to our own nature. The dishonesty to our self seems to

create the real problem. In this prescription we see the basic issue of

human problems. It involves not only the moral and ethical questions but

the fundamental question of our alienation from reality. The approach of

the I Ching to therapy is total and profound. It is more than psychologi-

cal. It deals with metaphysical questions as well. To follow the pre-

scription that the I Ching provides is to live according to it. In other

words, therapy deals with the way of life. We heal our maladjustment

by way of living rather than the instant treatment of symptom through

medication or shock treatment. Our way of life is actually the healing

process itself. Therefore, the I Ching is a book of self-healing, for

most of all it teaches the art of good living.

CHAPTER VII

THE I CHING AND THE NEW CONCEPT OF GOD

In the past the idea of God has been conceived as the unchanging being, which has been the basic characteristic of the ultimate reality. God as the unchanging reality has been clearly expressed in the Aristotelian notion of God as the "Immovable First Mover," which was refined by Thomas Aquinas in the middle ages. Aquinas, following the Aristotelian concept of God, defined the divine perfection in terms of unchanging being. Since God is perfect, "only God is altogether unchangeable: creatures can all change in some way or other."[1] Creatures change because they are imperfect. Being incomplete, they change toward the actualization of their potential becoming. However, God who is perfect both potentially and actually is not subject to the process of change. Even though Reformers such as Luther and Calvin rejected Aquinas' teachings, they did not make any attempt to alter his concept of God as the unchanging being. In fact to conceive of God as change or the "Moving Mover" is still unthinkable to most religious people in our time. The traditional definition of God as the "Unmoved Mover" is still relevant for most theologians of our time.

However, the concept of God can be altered if we alter the frame of reference by which we conceive the idea of God. Can God be understood as "Change-itself" rather than "Being-itself"? Can he be the "Moving Mover" rather than the "Unmoved Mover"? If we alter the frame of reference from the static and absolute to the dynamic and relative, it is possible to define God as "Change-itself" or the "Moving Mover." When we shift the basic frame of reference from the absolute to the relative, we have to reverse our thinking process; it is no longer the unchanging but the changing which makes things valuable. In this respect the I Ching alters the concept of God or the ultimate reality which we have been accustomed in the West. As we examine whether the concept of God defined by the I Ching is relevant to the Judeo-Christian concept of God, we will see that the concept of God as expressed in the Judeo-Christian faith is compatible with Change itself which takes the expression of the ultimate reality in the I Ching.

The God of Hebrews and Christians is known by many different names or symbols, such as "Lord," "Master," "Father," "King," "Creator," "Love," "Truth," "Spirit," and "Light." They are symbolic reflections of God under certain conditions of man's experience of the divine presence. Our inquiry into the concept of God in the Judeo-Christian faith must be based on the idea of God that existed before the symbolization of God in human terms.

The most primordial idea of God seems to be expressed in

Exodus 3:1-15 which describes the first confrontation between Moses

and God. In this confrontation God directed Moses to tell the people of

Israel that he was sent by the God of their fathers to liberate his people.

Moses answered, "If I come to the people of Israel and say to them,

'The God of your fathers has sent me to you,' and they ask me, 'What is

his name?', what shall I say to them?" God said to Moses, "I AM WHO

I AM" (Exodus 3:13-14). God also said to Moses, "Say this to the

people of Israel, 'The Lord (YHWH), the God of your fathers, the God

of Abraham, the God of Isaac, and the God of Jacob, has sent me to you'"

(Exodus 3:15). In these passages of Exodus, an unadorned description of

the God of the Judeo-Christian tradition is presented. Therefore, it is of

utmost importance for us to examine these passages clearly to compre-

hend the real meaning of the divine nature, paying particular attention to

the name of God, "I AM WHO I AM," which is used interchangeably with

"YHWH." Alternative translations of this phrase are "I AM WHAT I AM,"

"I WILL BE WHAT I WILL BE,"[2] and "I BECOME WHAT I BECOME."[3]

YHWH seems to derive from the Hebrew verb hayah, which can be trans-

lated as "to exist," "to become" or "is-ness."[4] Therefore, the meaning

of "I AM WHAT I AM" and "YHWH" is identical.

"I AM WHO I AM" or "I BECOME WHAT I BECOME" (ėhyeh áser

ėhyeh) is the most profound, yet the most ambiguous phrase which we encounter in the Old Testament. It is in fact a mystical statement, meaning that God is nameless, beyond human imagination and understanding. Words cannot express His nature. God is wholly other. As Jacob said, "God is found who in speaking of himself says: I am (éhyeh) and of whom men affirm: he is (yihyeh)."[5] Although God is without human attributes, yet the early Church attempted to define what God ought to be through the use of three persons and one substance. He is "mysterium logicum," the mystery that is beyond human conceptualization. Because God eludes human imagery, there is no adequate symbol for Him. We can only say that God is or God exists. What we know of God is only His is-ness, which is a non-symbolic statement, for it does not point beyond itself.[6] God as "is-ness itself" can transcend the dichotomy between opposites.

In the Upanishads this kind of nonsymbolic statement is attributed to the supreme reality. It transcends our senses and our thoughts: "There the eye goes not; speech goes not, nor the mind. We know not, we understand not how one would teach It."[7] This supreme reality cannot be described. "Not by speech, not by mind, not by sight can It be apprehended. How can It be comprehended otherwise than by one's saying 'It is!'"[8] Thus It is known through the famous formula of double negation "Neti, neti" (neither this nor that), which denies any human attributes that might adequately describe It. This supreme reality

transcends the differentiation between subject and object, and is Pure
Consciousness. Therefore, as far as the nonsymbolic nature of the
supreme reality is concerned, both Brahman and YHWH are identical.

The nonsymbolic nature of Nirvana is also affirmed in Buddhist
teachings. The idea of Nirvana is rather difficult to compare with the
Judeo-Christian idea of God.[9] Etymologically "Nirvana" means "to
extinguish," that is, to extinguish the causes of suffering. Thus, a
wanderer said to Reverend Sariputta: "Whatever, your reverence, is the
extinction of passion, of aversion, of confusion, this is called
Nirvana."[10] This condition of extinction is "incomprehensible,
indescribable, inconceivable, unutterable, for after we eliminate every
aspect of the only consciousness we now know, how can we speak of
what is left?"[11] In it "there is no coming or going or remaining or
deceasing or uprising, for this is itself without support, without con-
tinuance, without mental object--this is itself the end of suffering."[12]
Therefore, Nagasena attempts to illustrate the nonsymbolic nature of
Nirvana by using wind as an analogy. He begins with the question: "Is
there, sire, what is called wind?"

> "Yes, revered sir."
> "Please, sire, show the wind by its colour or configuration or
> as thin or long or short."
> "But it is not possible, revered Nagasena, for the wind to be
> shown; for the wind cannot be grasped in the hand or touched;
> but yet there is the wind."

"If, sire, it is not possible for the wind to be shown, well then, there is no wind."
"I, revered Nagasena, know that there is wind, I am convinced of it, but I am not able to show the wind."
"Even so, sire, there is Nirvana; but it is not possible to show Nirvana by colour or configuration."[13]

As Huston Smith said, "This indescribable character of Nirvana caused later Buddhists to speak of it as Śunyatā or Emptiness. It is not void or a negation of existence, but is empty in a way analogous to the way suprasonic is empty of sounds our ears can detect."[14] Therefore, the supreme reality in Buddhist tradition, whether it is Nirvana or Śunyatā, is expressed in nonsymbolic terms. As far as its nonsymbolic nature is concerned, it is identical with Brahman and YHWH.

In the Tao Te Ching, Tao or the ultimate reality is also described nonsymbolically. Lao Tzu begins with the nonsymbolic meaning of Tao: "The Tao that can be said is not the eternal Tao, and the name that can be named is not the real name." Tao in this respect is indescribable and incomprehensible. It is beyond the understanding of human wisdom. That is why one of the Tang poets, P'o Chu-i, of the ninth century, remarks on the Tao of Lao Tzu as follows:

Those who speak do not know;
Those who know do not speak.
This is what we were told by Lao Tzu.
Should we believe that he himself was the one who knew;
How could it then be that he wrote no less than five thousand
words.[15]

Lao Tzu knew that Tao's "is-ness" is a mystery. Thus Lao Tzu said,
"When you look at it, you cannot see it; it is called formless. When you
listen to it you cannot hear it; it is called soundless."[16] The Tao is a
void, used but never filled.[17] It is then similar to the notion of
Śūnyatā or Godhead as "pure nothingness" (ein bloss nicht).[18] As Lao
Tzu said, "Its true name we do not know; 'the Tao' (Brahman, Nirvana or
YHWH) is the byname we give it."[19] In this respect, the nonsymbolic
nature of God as "is-ness itself" seems to transcend all other names of
God. This notion of "is-ness" (isticheit) is clearly expressed in Japanese
as "sono-mama" (そのまま) which "transcends everything, it has no
moorings. No concepts can reach it, no understanding can grasp it."[20]
Thus, sono-mama, that is, "I am that I am," is the most profound statement of the mystery of God. Suzuki is certainly right when he said: "The
Biblical God is said to have given his name to Moses on Mount Sinai as
'I am that I am.' This is a most profound utterance, for all our religious
or spiritual or metaphysical experiences start from it."[21] God as "sono-
mama itself" or "is-ness itself" is the most primordial meaning of God
known in the Old Testament.

God as "is-ness itself" is not identical with Paul Tillich's definition
of God as "being itself." Even though the nonsymbolic description of God
is similar, their difference becomes obvious when we examine their
characteristic emphasis. The concept of God as "is-ness itself" stresses

the dynamic aspect of God, that is, the essence of changing process. On the other hand, the structural aspect of God is emphasized in "being itself."

In order to see the difference between "is-ness itself" and "being itself," we can begin with Tillich's understanding of the term "being itself" in relation to the unknown God. Tillich's interest in a "being" as well as "being itself" comes from the point of view of ontology: "As we already have seen, God as being-itself is the ground of the ontological structure of being without being subject to this structure himself."[22] His interest in it is clear: "God is the ground of the structure of being" and "he is the structure."[23] When Robert P. Scharlemann suggested a change from "God as being" to "God is," Tillich's response was not favorable.[24] Therefore, Tillich's definition of God as "being itself" is not in total agreement with the meaning of God in Exodus 3:1-15 in which the emphasis is on the verb "is" rather than the ontological structure of being. The name "YHWH" is directly connected with the verb "hayah," which means "to be" in an active and dynamic sense. Thus, God in Exodus 3:15 must be differentiated from God in the Platonic and Tillichian sense. "The verb hayah, when it refers to God," van Leeuwen said, "expresses his personal, dynamic, active being vis-a-vis his people and his creation."[25] Here the emphasis is on the dynamic action of becoming as opposed to Tillich's stress on the structure of being.

Moreover, the name "YHWH" seems to have its origin in the primitive notion of lightning and thunder, just as the concept of heaven (<u>Ch'ien</u> or 乾) in China was directly related to the power of the dragon, which was believed to manifest itself in lightning and thunder.[26] According to van Leeuwen, "The name 'Yahweh,' which is in origin Kenite or Ugaritic, takes us back to an indefinable power encountered in the lightning and thunder."[27] Jacob believes that "Yahweh in its primitive form <u>yah</u> was only originally an interjection, a kind of ejaculation uttered in moments of excitement and in connection with the moon cult; the complete name of Yahweh or Yahu would then be this interjection followed by the personal pronoun for the third person."[28] It seems then quite reliable to believe that the name "Yahweh" or "YHWH," which is used in the Old Testament "more than 6,700 times,"[29] is more closely associated with power or energy than with a structural being. Another name, "El," which is also commonly used, "expresses life in its power."[30] The literal meaning of the Hebrew word "El" or "Elohim" is "to be strong" or "to be mighty."[31] El is associated with the power in creation: "In the beginning God (i.e., Elohim) created the heaven and the earth" (Genesis 1:1). Therefore, El, God, is associated with the power of various objects, such as the mountains of El (Ps. 36:7), the cedars of El (Ps. 80:11), the stars of El (Is. 14:13) or the army of Elohim (I Chr. 12:22). Based on the evidence of God's primordial names, we must conclude that the concept of God in the beginning was more closely associated with the idea of power or energy which changes and transforms the world. "The Hebrew way of conceiving reality" is, as van Leeuwen said, "a changing, moving, affective, and dramatic whole."[32] Thus, to conceive of God as the structure of being is not in harmony with the spirit of the Hebrew way of conceiving the ultimate reality as "is-ness itself." God as "is-ness itself" (sono-mama or suchness) is primarily the power of change itself. Suzuki said, "The principle of Suchness is not static, it is full of dynamic forces."[33]

If God's is-ness is dynamic, can He be described in terms of "becoming itself"? "Is-ness itself" is more than "becoming itself." The idea of "becoming" cannot take the frame of the ultimate reality because of the intrinsic limitation of its meaning. In this respect, Tillich is right: "to speak of a 'becoming God' disrupts the balance between dynamics and form and subjects God open to the future and has the character of an absolute accident. In both cases the divinity of God is undercut."[34] The problem with "becoming" is, as Tillich attempts to point out, the inherent meaning of "not-yet," which not only limits the power of God but creates the never-ending process of becoming. Because of this intrinsic limitation of "not-yet" in becoming, it cannot express the ultimate reality.

If God cannot be "becoming itself," because "becoming" cannot

express the category of the ultimate, we must find a term which suggests

a deeper reality. If we define becoming as a process of creativity, there

must be something which makes this kind of process possible. In every

process of becoming there must be that which is more fundamental than

the process, since becoming is not an expression of the ultimate. The

fundamental description of God as "is-ness itself" is expressed in terms

of change, which will answer the "not-yet" element of becoming.

As we have already pointed out, becoming as the process of

creativity cannot express the ultimate. The I Ching seems to reassure

us of this limited character of creative becoming. The creative process

is possible because of the I (易) or Change, which changes and creates

everything in the world. Thus, becoming, that is, the process of

creativity, is subsidiary to Change. In the I Ching, the I or Change is

the begetter of heaven and earth.[35] Creativity is the characteristic of

heaven, while responsiveness is the characteristic of earth. The former

is symbolized in the first hexagram, Ch'ien (乾) or Creativity, and the

latter in the second hexagram, K'un (坤) or Responsiveness. The former

signifies the infinite concentration of yang energy, while the latter the

infinite concentration of yin energy. The hexagram Ch'ien consists of

yang or undivided lines only, while the hexagram K'un consists of yin or

divided lines only. They are complementary to one another and create and recreate everything in the world. Nothing can exist without them. However, these two primoridal essences owe their existence to Change, which is then the ultimate reality of all that is becoming and in process. Any process of becoming is ultimately attributed to the interplay of yin and yang forces. Yin and yang are the basic constituents of becoming. Since these two primary forces are conditioned by Change, Change is the basis of becoming and the creative process. Thus, the Great Commentary to the I Ching says, "The Great Ultimate (T'ai Chi 太極) is in Change. Change produces the two primary forms. The two primary forms produce the four images. The four images produce the eight trigrams."[36] Here, two primary forms signify Creativity (heaven) and Responsiveness (earth) or the prime yang and prime yin. Thus, the commentary remarks further: "Therefore: There are no greater primal images than heaven and earth."[37] By doubling both yin and yang lines, we get the four images: the old yang, young yin, old yin and young yang.[38] By adding another yin or yang line to the four images or duograms the eight trigrams are evolved. According to the I Ching, these eight symbols are the basis for everything in the universe. Here, we see the evolution of eight trigrams from the circle of the Great Ultimate, which is identified with Change in the Great Commentary of the I Ching. Fung Yu-lan believes that the diagram of the Great Ultimate (T'ai Chi T'u 太極圖), which was discovered by Chou Tun-i (1017-73), "became the first systematic product of Sung and Ming

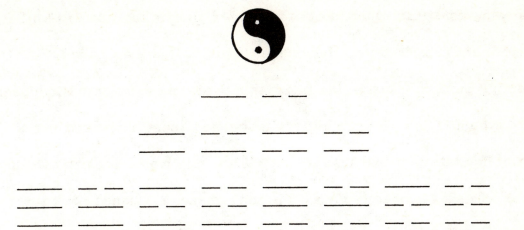

Neo-Confucianism."[39] Furthermore, in the I T'ung (Explanation of the

Change) Chou had in mind Change when he discussed the Great

Ultimate.[40]   Therefore, Ch'u Chai rightly points out, "The word I (or

Change) is used interchangeably with the word Tao, since Tao is life,

spontaneity, evolution, or in one word, change itself."[41] It is then

Change or Tao, which is also the Great Ultimate or Ultimate Reality,

that becomes the source of the evolutionary process of becoming. Just

as Change is the source of all creative becoming, Tao is the source of

all things. Thus, Lao Tzu said, "The Way (Tao) begot one, and the one,

two; then the two begot three and three all else."[42] Here, the Way or

Tao is Change, the source of one or creativity (heaven). Two means both

heaven and earth or creativity and responsiveness, which produce three

or the trigram, the basis of the hexagram. Since 64 hexagrams symbolize

the microcosm of the total universe, everything comes from trigrams.

Thus Hsi Tz'u, one of the Ten Wings of the I Ching, says, "One yin and one yang constitute what is called Tao."[43] Tao is the mother of all

things, and "the begetter of all begetting is called the Change."[44] The

creative process of becoming finds its ultimate expression in Change or

Tao, which is, as we have already discussed, best expressed in the non-

symbolic statement "is-ness itself." This statement becomes meaningful

to us when it is understood as signifying change. Change not only

qualifies the dynamic existence of God's "is-ness" but also is an

answer to the "not-yet" of creative becoming. In order to illustrate

God's "is-ness itself" as "change itself," let us use a turning wheel as

an analogy: God as "is-ness itself" occupies the center of this moving

wheel and the rest of the wheel represents the universe. This center or

axis is the core of the entire wheel, and its motion determines the move-

ments of all of its other parts. This axis causes the wheel to move by

moving itself, and therefore is analogous to Change or "change itself."

It is definitely not the "Unmoved Mover," but is the "Moving Mover" or

"Changing Changer," which is the source of all creative becoming. It

is not subject to becoming, even though it is in the becoming, for it is

the source of the becoming and changing process. That is why Suzuki

said, "The moving images of the eternal essence which alone 'is' and

not subject to becoming."[45] Change itself is then the most meaningful

expression of God's is-ness in the world of constant change and becoming.

Everything changes because of Change, but Change itself is changeless, for it is the "all-changing changeless."[46]

In conclusion let us review the argument which forms the main thesis of this discussion. In order to discover the primordial meaning of God in the Judeo-Christian faith, we have selected the text Exodus 3:1-15 which describes the initial contact between God and Moses. From an analysis of "I AM WHAT I AM" and "YHWH," we have indicated the God of YHWH to be incomprehensible, unknowable, and indescribable in any human terms. As far as this nonsymbolic nature of God is concerned, the Judeo-Christian God is identical with Brahman, Nirvana and Tao. We began with this nonsymbolic nature of God's existence as "is-ness itself" and attempted to find a more meaningful metaphysical affirmation of his "is-ness itself." As a result we examined Paul Tillich's definition of God as "being itself," which does not confront the reality of God's is-ness, even though it is a nonsymbolic statement about God. Tillich's idea of "being itself" emphasizes the structural form of being rather than the dynamic aspect of God. Therefore, we have concluded that God as "being itself" is not only contrary to the spirit of the Hebraic way of thinking but inconsistent with the basic characteristic of "is-ness" which is essentially dynamic. We considered the category of becoming as an alternative. However, it must be rejected because of its intrinsic limitation. The notion of becoming implies "not-yet," and undercuts the perfection and purity of "is-ness itself." The final stage

of our investigation was a search in the I Ching for the category that

would most meaningfully satisfy the process of becoming. According to

the I Ching, Change is not only the source of creative becoming but the

ultimate reality. Thus, the ultimate reality as "is-ness itself" can be

meaningfully expressed in terms of "change itself." God as "change

itself" is the source of every creative becoming. Just as the axis of a

moving wheel, the Change changes all parts of the wheel by changing

itself. Even though everything changes, the inmost core of changing

process is changeless. Thus, Tao Te Ching says, "Essential nature

(Ming) is everchanging-changeless" (Ch. 16). In other words, "The

mystery of change is precisely 'Change that is the changeless.'"[47] To

understand God's "is-ness" we have to understand," said Chang Chung-

yuan, "the concept of the changeless within the ever-changing."[48]

What is then the real meaning of changelessness if God is change

itself? If God is changing reality, how does this affect the steadfastness

of God in his relations with his people? How does it alter the profound

convictions of the Hebrew prophets on the changelessness of God?

Malachi said, "I the Lord do not change" (Malachi 3:6). This view was

shared by the Psalmist who declared: "They will perish, but thou dost

endure; they will all wear out like a garment. Thou changest them like

raiment, and they pass away; but thou art the same, and thy years have

no end" (Ps. 102:26-27). We see many similar affirmations in the New
Testament about the changelessness of God. For example, in the
Epistle of Hebrews, it is said, "Jesus Christ is the same yesterday and
today and forever" (Hebrews 13:8). If God does not have the characteristic of changelessness, his people cannot trust in him. However, we
must understand that the changelessness of God does not imply a static
and frozen statue who cannot move. Instead, it reinforces the idea of
the consistency and steadfastness of God's will. In other words, the
character of changelessness is a part of the changing reality of God:
changelessness is possible because of change. God is changeless
because he is primarily change itself. Changelessness means, then,
the changeless pattern of change, or consistent structural change. It is
a structural form of Change. The changelessness of God does not negate
his essential nature as Change but affirms the pure form of changing
activity. It is the purity of change which makes changelessness possible,
and therefore the element of changelessness is found within the change
itself. "The Taoist would say that the flying arrow represents the changeless within the everchanging . . . . The arrow moves all the time, but at
the same time it does not move at all. To quote the Buddhists: 'Though
things move, they are forever motionless; though things are motionless,
they do not cease moving.'"[49] Changelessness is then the pure form of
change which makes change constant and regular. Thus, "The constancy

and regularity of changes are the very essence of the eternal and invariable principle of change."[50] As John C. Murray said, "Over against the inconstancy and infidelity of the people, who continually absent themselves from God, the name Yahweh affirms the constancy of God, but unchangeable fidelity to this promise of presence. Malachi, the last of the prophets, stated this first facet of the primitive revelation: 'I (am) Yahweh; I do not change' (3:5)."[51] Changelessness is then primarily his faithfulness to himself, that is, "change itself."

If God is not Change in the changing world, he is not in the world. If God is only the "Unmoved Mover" in the moving universe, he is not a part of the universe. He is only an observer, not a participant in history. Leslie Dewart states this point in a figurative manner. "God does not dip his finger into history; he totally immerses himself in it. When he visits the world he does not come slumming. He comes to stay. He arrives most concretely and decisively of all in the person of the Word in order to make earth and history his home, his permanent residence."[52] If God is concretely in the world of change and transformation, the changing God is more compatible with concrete religious experience than the absolute, unchanging and timeless Being of traditional theology.[53] The God of unchanging Being in the changing cosmos is not only inconsistent but contrary to his essence as the life-giver and life-receiver. God as "change itself" reaffirms his role as both life-giver and life-receiver. He is the center or the inmost core of the changing world as well as the source of the creative process of becoming. The cosmos is living and changing because of the living and changing God, who is the ground of all things. It is this dynamic God, who is finally responsible for the living and changing universe. As Pittenger said, "the only reasonable explanation of the living cosmos is in fact the living God."[54] To deny the idea of a changing God is to deny the living God, because the living organism is always in the process of change. There is no way to separate the world and God. Even the concept of Nirvana cannot exist independent of the world of change. "Nirvana is another name for the Emptiness (Śūnyatā),"[55] but it is more than a pure form. It is also "what makes all these things possible; it is a zero full of infinite possibilities, it is a void of inexhaustible contents."[56] Therefore, "Nirvana is samsara and samsara is Nirvana."[57] Following the teaching of Prajñāpāramitā-sūtra, Suzuki attempts to describe the inseparableness of the infinite from the finite and God's "is-ness" from our "is-ness." He quotes Eckhart's words, "God's is-ness is my is-ness and neither more nor less."[58] God as "is-ness itself" is inseparable from the world as "is-ness." If the world is constantly changing and becoming as the theory of relativity and nuclear science have suggested, God must be the subject of this change. Therefore, the world view of our time almost forces us to believe in the changing God.

God is changeless because He is primarily Change itself. The everchanging nature of God has in himself the unchanging patterns of change. Thus God is both changing and changeless at the same time. Ogden sums up this point in this remark: "_That_ he is ever-changing is itself the product or effect of no change whatever, but is in the strictest sense changeless, the immutable ground of change as such, both its own and others."[59] The God who transcends the conflict between subject and object is "change itself" which is also changeless. "The unchanging aspect of _Tao_ (or God)," as Donald Munro says, "is compared to the center _shu_ [樞] of a wheel. It is hollow, and hence contains only nothingness [_wu_ 無 or _Śūnyatā_]; but its very hollowness allows the wheel to turn on a shaft and thus be effective."[60] God as "change itself" is, then, the heart of the change and the eternal change. Thus, Swami Prabhavananda says, "Endless change without, and at the heart of the change an abiding reality--_Brahman_. Endless change within, and at the heart of the change an abiding reality--_Ātman_ . . . . _Brahman_ and _Ātman_ are one and the same. And they summed up the prodigious affirmation in the words _Tat_ _Tvam_ _asi_--That thou art."[61] We may also sum up our understanding of the nonsymbolic description of God as "change itself" or the "heart of change" which is changeless.

CHAPTER VIII

THE I CHING AND BEYOND NEW MORALITY

The growing interest of the West in the Book of Changes or the

I Ching has brought special attention to the problem of moral and ethical

questions. Since the book had been popularly regarded as a manual of

divination, it has aroused considerable suspicions as to its moral and

ethical relevance in the life of the West. These suspicions might be

derived from the idea that there must be some kind of correlation between

the moral practices of the Western people and the concepts presented in

the I Ching. It is possible that the book contains profound insights

which happen to correspond with what the Western people have been

searching for. Whatever the case might be, the book seems to satisfy

their emotional and intellectual upsurges toward the search for new mean-

ing and existence in their life-style. If the values for which the people

of our time are searching are found in the I Ching, there must be some

correlations between the value orientations of the West in our time and

those of this archaic book. However, this kind of assumption does not

always lead to the conclusion that the moral teachings found in the

I Ching are identical with those of the West in our generation. What I

143

attempt to do here is to show that there are enough similarities between the new morality of our time and the old morality of the I Ching. In other words, new morality is not really new but the renewal of the old. Moreover, the new morality of our time in the West is not as radical as the old morality prescribed in the I Ching, one of the Confucian classics in China.

Anyone acquainted with the I Ching will soon come to notice that it is not a textbook of ethical and moral teachings. It is full of symbols and cryptic sayings of old China dealing with all sorts of affairs and imaginations; however, ethical and moral implications are found within the frame of these symbolic and cryptic expressions. Thus it is our task to search for moral implications presented in the total context of this book.

The moral issues which the I Ching presupposes ought to be seen in the light of "I" or change, which is the core of this book. Since it is the change which changes all things, everything, except the change itself, is relative to change. Because even ethical and moral theory is relative to change, it cannot be absolute in any sense. Thus the I Ching presupposes ethical relativism. It is not possible to assert any absolutistic moral and ethical values in the light of constant change and transformation of all things in the universe. No ethical and moral principles are absolute. They are relative to time and situation because of constant change. No law is absolute in itself. Legalism is totally alien to the ethical theory which the I Ching presupposes. It is an ethical theory which does not necessitate any law. It is then a genuine form of situation ethics or contextual ethics in the purest form. It is the given situation which dictates the ethical decision. It is not the law which demands our decision regardless of a given situation. All ethical and moral decisions are to be made in relation to the particular context in which the issues are presented.

The relativistic and contextual significance of ethical and moral issues is clearly expressed in the very nature of the hexagrams themselves. The hexagrams are understood as the archetypical or germinal situations for all things, including ethical and moral questions. Each moral situation represented by a particular hexagram(s) is peculiar to itself, even though its autonomy is possible only in its relation to other hexagrams. In other words, each hexagram(s) attained through tossing coins or dividing yarrow stalks represents its own ethical and moral situation that is not contained in any other hexagrams. Therefore, the germinal situation or hexagram is valid only in that particular issue expressed in that particular situation of time and place. In this respect, it is not the general principle but the particular situation that provides the meaningful process of moral and ethical decisions. Since a situation represented by a hexagram is not absolute but relative to other hexagrams, the moral theory that the _I Ching_ presupposes is not only situational but relativistic in character.

We may believe situation ethics is the frontier movement of Western thinking in our time, but it was already implicit in the _I Ching_. Perhaps the ethical theory which the _I Ching_ presupposes is the most thorough-going contextual ethics which has ever been known in the history of mankind. How radical situation ethics in our time might be, it cannot be more radical than that which the _I Ching_ presupposes. In this sense the contemporary movement of ethical situationalism is nothing but the renewal of the old ethics of the _I Ching_.

However, the uniqueness of ethical and moral theory which the _I Ching_ presupposes is much more than mere situation ethics. It is also complementary ethics, based on the complementary relationship between opposites. Since change takes place according to the complementary relationship of opposites, ethical and moral theory is no exception to this kind of relationship. Complementary ethics means that the opposing ethical values are not dichotomous but complementary. What is good is complementary to evil, and what is evil fulfills what is good. Nothing is absolutely self-sustaining. No value is absolute in itself. Thus we must deny any value judgment to be absolute. What is good is due to evil, and what is evil is due to good in an ultimate sense. Thus values are not only relative to situations but also to their counterparts. What is right is due

to wrong and what is wrong is due to right, because they are in a complementary relationship. Just as yin is not without yang and yang is
not without yin, what is good is not without evil and what is evil is not
without good. Thus good and evil are ultimately inseparable. Even
though they are opposite in character, they are one. Thus Lao Tzu says,
"Surely the good man is the bad man's teacher; and the bad man is the
good man's business. If the one does not respect his teacher, or the
other does not love his business, his error is very great" (Tao Te Ching,
Ch. 27). Again, he states, "Bad fortune will promote the good. Good
fortune, too, gives rise to bad" (Tao Te Ching, Ch. 57). These ethical
statements made by Lao Tzu are not strange to the ideas expressed in the
I Ching. Lao Tzu presupposes the Tao as the background of the change,
the change that is changeless. As Ta Chuan says, "Its tao is forever
changing" (Sec. II, Ch. 8). Again it says further the Tao as the background of the change: "The Tao is the change and movement" (Sec. II,
Ch. 10). Since change, the foreground of Tao, is possible through the
complement of the opposites, ethical and moral values are also possible
through the complementary relationship of the opposing values. What is
good or what is bad are only phenomenal distinctions. They are
essentially parts of the whole. They are essentially one and inseparable.
Thus the I Ching presents ethical monism in a thoroughgoing fashion.
Ethical dualism which we cling to is phenomenologically conditioned.

Thus the ethical theory which the I Ching prescribes is not only contextual but complementary. The morality of the I Ching goes much further
than the new morality of our time in the West. According to the I Ching,
ethical decisions are not only relative to given situations but also to
values for which the decisions are to be made.

Even though the ethical theory which the I Ching presupposes is a
thoroughgoing form of relativistic morality, there must be a norm or the
norm for our decision as to the choice of good or bad, even though the
decision is not in any sense ultimate. For example, the norm for decisions
in Christian situational ethics is love. As Fletcher says, "The ultimate
norm of Christian decision is love: nothing else."[1] Love then becomes
the criterion for ethical decision in new morality. However, the I Ching,
unlike the Christian Bible, says it is not love but the Tao, the principle
of natural harmony and peace, which gives values to all things. The Tao
or the Way makes things natural, and what is natural is in harmony.
Harmony is then the criterion for good. Since harmony is natural, what
is good is also natural. What is not natural is then evil. Both what is
natural and what is unnatural are only existential differentiations, just
as what is good and evil are phenomenological distinctions. Here, the
ontology and the axiology of the I Ching are correlated with each other.

One may object to the ethical principle which the I Ching prescribes
as natural ethics. G. E. Moore, for example, makes a strong case

against natural ethics by saying that "good itself can be defined by reference to such a property as naturalistic."[2] He attacks it further: "If everything natural is equally good, then certainly ethics, as it is ordinarily understood, disappears."[3] Joseph Fletcher likewise denounces natural ethics: "It (naturalistic ethics) suggests whatever situation at any time exists is good; that whatever is, is good. That is meaningless in ethics, if not in every other forum."[4] However, it is a grave mistake to identify the ethics of the I Ching with the naturalistic ethics which the Western mind coins. Even though the former may correspond to one's naturalistic disposition, it is quite different from the naturalistic ethics which Fletcher and Moore attack. The ethics of the I Ching never "suggests whatever situation at any time exists is good." It is more thorough-going situation ethics than Fletcher suggests, as we have already pointed out. Moreover, the ethics which the I Ching presupposes is not based on what is natural. What is natural is possible because of the change, which is the norm of ethical principle. In other words, the change, the foreground of Tao, is the source of good, the quality of naturalness. That is why it is more than naturalistic ethics. It is in fact transcendental ethics, for it transcends naturalistic value orientations. It is not the naturalness, but the change, which gives value to things. What is natural is the disposition of good because of harmony, which is the way of change. Harmony is then the sign of good, while disharmony, that is, self-assertion, is the sign of evil. Let us look at the hexagram 11,

T'ai or Peace. It means peace and goodness, because of the symbol of

```
 — —
 — —
 — —
 ———
 ———
 ———
```

harmonious relationship between K'un, or earth, and Ch'ien, or heaven.

The trigram Ch'ien, which is a light principle, moves upward; and the

trigram K'un, which is a heavy principle, moves downward. Thus both of

them meet each other in harmony. Because there is harmony, there is

peace; and peace brings good fortune and success. Since harmony is

based on the complementary relationship of the opposites, as we have

seen in hexagram 11, Confucius defines the idea of reciprocity as the

norm of ethical principles.

If the ultimate norm of our ethical decisions is based on the way of

change, how do we know the way? If we define the way of change as the

principle of harmony, that is, the underlying power of natural order, our

ethical decision must be based on this primordial power of harmony in a

final analysis. However, as we have already pointed out, this power of

order is the inner will, which seems to function independently from the

external desire or rational reference. This inner will which the I Ching describes is then independent of our conscious action. In other words, the guideline for our ethical action must be the activity of our unconsciousness. To be inward means to be spontaneous, and to be spontaneous means to be unconscious of self. Thus the act of inner will means the act of unconsciousness. The unconscious becomes the subject of our ethical decisions. The act of our unconsciousness is possible through the use of divination, the means of selecting the ethical situations. Divination is then a means to select a certain guideline for ethical decisions. Thus divination takes a legitimate place in the ethics which the I Ching presupposes. Since the ethical guideline is selected through the use of divination, it is quite different from the rational or conscious ethics to which we are accustomed.

Divination as a means of selecting the ethical guideline presupposes that the unconscious self is an inseparable part of man's total self. The I Ching views the whole man as the combination of both the conscious and the unconscious. Since the unconscious self is an intrinsic part of oneself, the use of divination, that is, the use of unconscious activity, in his ethical decision is perfectly acceptable. Furthermore, the I Ching regards the unconscious self as the subject of the conscious self. For this to be so, the unconscious self must become an important part in one's moral life. Because the unconscious self is the subject of the conscious self, it has a right to establish a certain guideline for the final decision of the conscious self. In this way the activity of subject self or unconscious self through the use of divination delimits the activity of object self or conscious self. The former sets up a clear guideline for the concrete decision of the latter. In this respect, the ethical decision of the conscious self is conditioned by that of the unconscious self, for the former is relative to the latter.

The uniqueness of ethics which the I Ching presupposes lies not simply in the use of divination. The I Ching does not use the divining process as a means of ethical decisions, even though it is true to many other divinations. The I Ching makes use of divination as a means to selecting the guidelines for concrete decisions. In other words, it gives room for the conscious self to make a concrete decision as to the moral and ethical choices at the end. Divination is a means to activate our unconsciousness which provides us a frame of reference. This frame of reference is the ethical guideline, which is known as the germinal situation in the hexagram. Divination does not make a final decision for moral responsibilities. It simply provides the trend or the movement of ethical situation by which our actual decisions are to be made. The unconscious self through the use of divination provides the background of the conscious self to make the concrete and final decision as to his moral responsibility. Therefore, the ethics of the I Ching brings together in terms of complementary relationship both the unconscious activity, which provides the ethical guideline, and the conscious activity, which

makes the final and actual decision. The activity of unconsciousness is

terminated by the activity of consciousness, and the latter is possible

because of the former. The use of both conscious and unconscious

activities in ethical and moral decision-making makes the ethics of

I Ching unique. Let us take an example to illustrate the relationship

between the conscious and unconscious activities in our ethical decision-

making. In order to select a guideline for our concrete decision for moral

issues involved, we have manipulated the yarrow stalks according to the

rule specified in the I Ching. Through the manipulation of the stalks our

unconsciousness is activated. The result of our manipulation which is

identical with the decision of our unconscious will, is supposed to be

symbolized by the hexagram 25, Wu Whang or Innocence. The Judgment

on this hexagram reads, "Wu Whang has great success. It is advantageous

```
 —————
 —————
 —————
 —— ——
 —— ——
 —————
```

to be firm. If you are not as you should be, you will get misfortune, and

it is not advantageous for you to undertake anything." As we see, the

judgment as expressed in this hexagram is not the concrete decision but only a guideline for our conscious action. It is simply an indication

which signifies the trend of ethical situation. It is analogous to an

ethical teaching at this particular circumstance. This ethical teaching

or guideline cannot be applied to other situations. It is relevant to this

particular situation alone.

As a result we notice that the I Ching presents the importance of

our unconscious activity in the matter of ethical decisions. Our con-

scious mind has very little to do in the actual decision-making process,

even though it is an intrinsic part of the whole. It is then quite different

from the process of ethical decision which we have been accustomed to in

Western civilization. In most cases wo do not give any attention to our

unconscious activity in the matter of our decision-making process.

However, as Carl Jung has pointed out, our experience shows that most

of our decisions are being made unconsciously. In most cases our moral

decisions are made more on the basis of our intuition than on our reason-

ing. The I Ching attempts to tell us that our unconscious mind is more

active than our conscious mind in the matter of our ethical and moral

decisions. Since our unconscious will does not always differ from our

conscious will, what we think of rational and conscious decision might

be the decision of our unconsciousness also. However, what the I Ching

attempts to say in the matter of moral decisions is important. It expands the realm of ethics to beyond our conscious activity. Perhaps its weakness is, in fact, its undue emphasis on our unconscious activity.

One may question whether the ethics of the I Ching allow any real freedom of choice or not. If our ethical decisions are guided by the unconscious, do we have freedom of choice? The I Ching will say, "Yes. You have freedom, the real freedom." Freedom for the I Ching means to be in harmony with the unconscious will, that is, the state of spontaneity without any external restriction or conscious awareness. Real freedom is found in the complete detachment of oneself from external desires and the passion of objectification. Freedom comes from the unconscious, for it is liberation from conscious activity. Thus, the decision of unconsciousness is a free choice, while the decision of consciousness is conditioned. In this respect the I Ching justifies its stand on the freedom of choice, which is essential to any ethical or moral theory.

Another question has to do with the concept of responsibility. Are we responsible for the decision we have made through the use of the divining process? The I Ching may say again, "You are responsible, for it is your own choice." The I Ching believes that man is more than a mere conscious self. He is both the conscious and unconscious self at the same time. The unconscious self is the subject of man, and the conscious self is the object of him. Thus what is chosen by the subject self through the use of divination is certainly as much responsible as what is chosen by the object or conscious self through the use of reason. Here again the I Ching opens up the transcendental category of ethical and moral responsibility.

Finally, let us consider moral virtues suggested in the I Ching, virtues which the I Ching implies are many but are relative to the excellence of yin and yang relationships. All virtues in their final sense are reduced to the quality of both yin and yang or creativity and responsivity. It is not the natural disposition that decides the nature of virtues. For example, it is not more virtuous to be a male than to be a female. It is not more virtuous to be the disposition of yang than to be that of yin. Virtue does not lie in ontic distinction but rather in functional excellence. What makes the male virtuous is the cultivation of the quality of creativity. What makes the female virtuous is the excellence of her disposition to be genuinely receptive. The I Ching denies that the very nature of yang is more valuable than that of yin. Since they are in complementary relation, one cannot be more valuable than the other.

The excellence of both yin and yang makes all other virtues possible. Among many kinds of virtues there are four cardinal ones, which are inherent in the first and second hexagrams. They are yuan (元) or originating and great, heng (享) or penetrating, li (利) or advantageous, and chen (貞) or correct. These four cardinal virtues represent the foundations of moral life in early China. <u>Yuan</u> or originating represents the excellence of <u>jen</u> (仁), which means empathy or magnanimous love. <u>Heng</u> or penetrating represents the excellence of <u>li</u> (禮), which means the propriety of ceremony. <u>Li</u> or advantageous represents the excellence of <u>i</u> (義), which means the act of righteousness. <u>Chen</u> or correctness represents the excellence of <u>chih</u> (質), which means substance. To summarize the four virtues, they are the excellences of <u>jen</u> (empathy), <u>li</u> (propriety), <u>i</u> (righteousness), and <u>chih</u> (substance). The cultivation of these four cardinal qualities, which are inherent in the very nature of man, makes the four cardinal virtues possible. These four cardinal virtues appear more than one hundred eighty times in both the judgments of hexagrams and the lines of hexagrams. Even though they are not identical with the four cardinal virtues of Greek philosophy, their basic implication, that is, the achievement of excellency, is very much similar to the Aristotelian notion of virtues. However, the concept of virtues in the <u>I Ching</u> seems to resemble the Stoic notion that virtues reside in living according to nature. Virtue lies in harmonious existence with the <u>Tao</u>, the universal law of harmony and order. It is this inner harmony with the process of change, the foreground of <u>Tao</u>, that makes all virtuous.

CHAPTER IX

THE I CHING AND NEW STYLES OF LIVING

The I Ching is more than a book which satisfies mere intellectual curiosities for Western people. It can change styles of living, as it has done for Far Eastern people in the past. However, this does not mean that the I Ching is going to answer all the problems that contemporary man confronts in his daily life. Braden is right, "One must seriously doubt that all of the answers to the contemporary American crisis can be found in the Book of Changes."[1] The I Ching can, however, give us some new styles of living that eventually help us to overcome the actual crises of our time.

What are the new styles of living that the I Ching can offer to contemporary man in the post-modern society? First of all it can offer cooperation rather than the competition that we have been accustomed to for centuries. The competitive way of living divides us from left to right, above and below, or from the rich to the poor. It is a device that breaks down opposites rather than bringing them together into harmonious cooperation. It creates the fear and anxieties of human civilization. It threatens every walk of life. In this kind of life-style we have to fight for our survival. Competition produces enormous emotional problems. It is based on the idea of conflicting dualism, on struggle as the inevitable way of life, which has been the dominant world view of the West for a long time. It promotes the strong and destroys the weak. It is conditioned by the exclusive way of thinking, the either-or way of thinking in the past.

The I Ching provides another style of living, the cooperative style, which does not divide. Rather it promotes the unity of both the inferior and the superior, both the strong and the weak, both the black and the white, and both the rich and the poor. It is interested in the complementary relation of opposites for the enrichment of the entire society. The cooperative life-style is the answer to the restless mind of our time. It can mend the wound of technical civilization and give deeper meaning to human existence. In this kind of life no member is excluded from the whole. However insignificant one might be, he is indispensable for the benefit of the whole. This kind of life-style creates the genuine community, the community of empathy, which is similar to the organic body. This view is central to Weltanschauung of the I Ching. The organic view of the cosmos, where everything complements for the sake of the whole, is strikingly similar to the New Testament concept of the Church. In Paul's letter to the Corinthians he describes the ideal community of believers in Christ:

> For as the body is one, and hath many members, and all the
> members of that one body, being many, are one body: so
> also is Christ. For by one Spirit are we all baptized into one
> body, whether we be Jews or Gentiles, whether we be bond or
> free; and have been all made to drink into one Spirit . . . .
> And those members of the body, which we think to be less
> honourable, upon these we bestow more abundant honour; and
> our uncomely parts have more abundant comeliness. For our
> comely parts have no need: but God hath tempered the body
> together, having more abundant honour to that part which
> lacked: That there should be no schism in the body; but that
> the members should have the same care one for another. And
> whether one member suffer, all the members suffer with it; or
> one member be honoured, all the members rejoice with it.
> Now ye are the body of Christ, and members in particular
> (I Corinthians 12:12-27).

Like the body of Christ, the human society which the I Ching presupposes

is analogous with the organic body, where one is complemented by the

other. The competitive society cannot be organic because it does not

allow the opposites to coexist together. Therefore, the cooperative style

of life is not only desirable for contemporary man but inevitable for the

solution of crises which converge in the present predicament. All the

possible resources of our time must be brought together for the higher

synthesis of a new and better community of all mankind. The cooperative

life-style can build up a higher form of civilization in the long run, while

the competitive style of life may work well for a while but be destructive

in the long run. Therefore, the new style of our lives ought to be coop-

erative, a mode that will meet the coming of the global community.

The _I Ching_ also teaches that the liberation of woman is essential

for the cooperative life-style of modern man. This contemporary

phenomenon is inevitable in the light of the complementary relationship

of yin and yang. The liberation of woman which the _I Ching_ teaches sheds

a significant light on the understanding of the man and woman relation-

ship. The _I Ching_ denies that man and woman are the same but asserts

that they are equal. Yin, woman, is equally significant to yang, man,

because the former is essential to the latter. We have already illustrated

their relationship in the diagram of the Great Ultimate where the opposites

are mutually intertwined together; man and woman are inseparable wholes.

Therefore, the liberation of woman is at the same time the liberation of

man. The inseparable relationship between man and woman must be

understood clearly in order to comprehend the nature of the woman's

liberation movement. This man-woman continuum is, as we have indi-

cated, based on the relationship of one and two, which derives from the

interplay of yin and yang in the _I Ching_. This inseparable union of man

and woman is found mostly in primitive civilizations. As Eliade says,

"In his immediate experience, man is made up of pairs of opposites."[2]

We also observe the inseparable union of two opposite sexes in count-

less statues of Hindu divine images. In Siberia and Korea, the shamans

usually assume both sexes. The male shaman wears the female dress,

and the female shaman wears the male dress. Both sexes are thus

162

brought together, with the shaman overcoming the conflicting dualism.

This idea is more clearly illustrated in the linear symbols of yin and

yang or the divided line (— —) and the undivided line (———) in the

I Ching. The divided line symbolizes the female sex, which is charac-

terized by openness, and the undivided line is symbolized by the male

organ which is characterized by straightness. As we notice, their

difference is conditioned by separation and union. Just as separation

presupposes union and union presupposes separation, man has woman

and woman has man. The inseparable relationship between the male and

female or yin and yang is clearly expressed in young yin (═ ═) and

young yang (═ ═). The former is yin or woman but contains yang (the

undivided line) or man. The latter is yang or man but contains yin

(divided line) or woman. Thus yin has yang and yang has yin, just as

woman has man and man has woman. This idea is known in Carl Jung's

concept of animus, man in woman, and anima, woman in man. If man is

in woman and woman is in man, the liberation of woman is also the

liberation of man. The oppression of woman is also the oppression of

man. When man degrades woman, he actually degrades himself. There-

fore, the I Ching teaches that the equality of woman with man is an

inherent quality that cannot be taken away. Thus woman's liberation is

to restore the original right which has been taken away by the male

dominated society in the past.

However, the I Ching also teaches that woman is not the same with man in her function. Woman is more yin or more feminine than man, and man is more masculine than woman. The function of yin and yang cannot be identical. If it were, the process of change would not take place. Yin is yin; yang is yang. Yin is passive, perceptive, tender, etc., while yang is active, creative, firm, etc. Each of them has different attributes. If we examine the value numbers of yin and yang in the process of divination, yin consists of two, and yang of three.[3] The ratio of yin and yang is 2:3. Thus the female and male relationship is asymmetrical, because of their functional difference. This functional difference of woman from man must be taken seriously in the woman's liberation movement. When we advocate equality of woman we mean equal right or status but not equal function. The denial of the feminine characteristic is in fact the denial of her own self. When the functional difference of woman is not realized, she loses her intrinsic nature. She is no longer woman who can complement man. The same thing is applicable to the function of man. When man fails to function as the masculine ought to do, he loses the intrinsic nature of his own self. He cannot complement woman for the complete manhood. Thus the functional distinction, that is, eventually, the distinction of roles between man and woman, must be retained. The confusion of roles between the opposites creates unnecessary problems in our time. It is the basis of the anxiety and hidden conflict in our lives. The clear definition of roles between man and woman is implicit in the process of change in the I Ching. This definition of roles must be transferred to our social and individual lives. Thus the liberation of woman is not her liberation from the roles which belong to her by nature. Rather it means her liberation from the value system which oppresses her attributes.

What is needed in our time is then not to change the roles of woman but to change the value system which is almost completely oriented toward the functional attributes of man. We value the active, firm, strong, positive, etc., which are the male characteristics. On the other hand, we devalue the feminine characteristics, such as the passive, yielding, weak, negative, etc. Just as yin is no less valuable than yang, the feminine characteristics are no less valuable than the male characteristics. Just as the negative is as valuable as the positive in the whole, the function of woman is as valuable as that of man. We must restore the values that are characteristic to woman. In other words, we must value the passive, yielding, negative, etc. as much as the active, firm, positive, etc. Unless the feminine or yin values are elevated to the male values, the liberation of woman is not completed. The restoration of a sound value system, which accommodates both the male and female characteristics, is the real liberation of woman and man.

The new life-style which the I Ching teaches also goes beyond the structure of technological science. We begin to see that technology controls our lives. Thoreau's warning that "we have become the tools of our own tools" has become real. We have become the slave of our own creatures. Many important decisions have been made due to technology, which demands our service. We have been trained for the machine, so that it becomes the center of our existence. We are often required to meet the demands of technology, rather than having technology meet our demands. Therefore, we have lost our authentic existence. Our existence is almost completely dependent on technology. We have experienced the complete blackout of electricity and the shortage of energy. We see how helpless we are when technology ceases operation. Even a clerk who checks out the goods in a store does not know what to do when the adding machine suddenly stalls. We are so dependent on technology that we have lost our own power to exist without our own creations.

The I Ching does not reject technology itself but rejects the dominance of our lives by technology. There is evidence of technological symbols in the I Ching. There are at least two hexagrams which are related to man-made instruments: The fiftieth hexagram Ting (鼎) or the Caldron, and the forty-eighth hexagram Ching (井) or the Well. The caldron here represents the sacrificial vessel to hold the cooked food in the temple of ancestors and at special banquets. It is the symbol of sacrifice and service. The well is to supply the water for the nourishment of the community. In early days a community was centered around the well (public). It is, like the caldron, made for the service of man's essential needs. Both of them deal with the primitive technology but were never intended to overpower man. They were made to serve man.

How does the I Ching help us to live beyond the power of technologism? It is possible to overcome the contamination of our lives by technological power through the complementary power provided by the I Ching. In other words, the power of technologism is overcome with the power of anti-technologism. This power of anti-technologism is strongly suggested in the I Ching. One of the basic characteristics of technologism in our day is end production. Technologism concerns itself with the end without the means. Because we are slaves of technologism, we are judged on the basis of our productivity. The more we produce the better persons we are. The quantity becomes more important than the quality. This kind of life-style is based on the power of technologism. The I Ching provides a new life-style which stresses the means rather than the end product, providing the complementary element of technologism. As we have already pointed out, what is most important in the divination process is not the answer itself but the actual process of manipulating yarrow stalks or tossing coins. The real significance of divination that the I Ching teaches is the means itself. In this respect it is

self-defeating to put the I Ching into a computer. To push the button to
find the proper hexagrams through a computer not only goes against the
genuine spirit of the I Ching but contaminates the purity of intention,
which is manifested in the actual process of divination itself. Thus we
see the similar stress in the Bhagavad Gita, one of the most important
Hindu Scriptures: "On action alone be thy interest, never on its fruits;
let not the fruits of action be thy motive, nor be thy attachment to
inaction (II.47)." Technologism contaminates life because it concerns
the fruits of action alone. The technological man is haunted by the production which takes away the joy of action or doing and living. When
we are contaminated by the fruits of action we cannot live authentically.
Our minds are constantly preoccupied with the goal or end in itself. The
I Ching stresses the means of action which complements the fruits of
action. Thus we can overcome the power of technologism through the
teachings of the I Ching.

Technology makes things complex. The advancement of technical
civilization is often understood in terms of the complexity of evolvements.
The higher we evolve in technology, the more complex we become. The
technological civilization has created a highly complex society, which
our lives turn in all directions. We are restless, anxious and unable to
calm down our inner selves. Complexity which technology has created
demands a greater burden of our involvement in external things rather than

in the inner world of our selves. The civilization full with anxiety and frustration is a mark of complexity, which is the externalizing process that creates tension and estrangement between the inner and outer selves. Complexity is also a process of division and separation, which is fundamental to the analytical approach of scientific method. In this respect the complexity that technological civilization creates eventually alienates the world from the true nature of our existence. Thus, the men of technologism are lonely in a crowd, isolated from the ground of their beings. They have lost authentic existence.

The I Ching overcomes the complexity that technology has created through the complementary power of simplicity. The fundamental concept of I or Change is, as we have already pointed out, simplicity and ease. Simplicity is the characteristic of Tao or Change, which eternally returns to its origin.[4] This origin or the root is the ultimate reality of change itself. All the complex phenomena are internalized in the I Ching and symbolized by the simplest images of broken and unbroken lines or yin and yang lines, which explains every possible process of becoming. Since all complex phenomena are reduced into yin and yang interaction, change which deals with this action is simple. The way of simplicity is the way of detachment, while that of complexity is attachment to the world. Simplicity is a characteristic of inner process, while complexity is the process of externalization. Simplicity is a basic attribute of wholeness, where unity is maintained. It is then the way of unity and inward realization. It is the way of liberated man who overcomes the burden of life created by technologism. Through simplicity the complexity of life is overcome, for the former complements the latter.

Technologism also contaminates our taste; we love artificial creations more than natural existence. Technology always deals with artificiality. Thus the man of technologism lives the artificial life, which is superficial, imitative, and inauthentic. Inauthentic objects replace authentic presences. Real flowers are replaced with artificial flowers, natural objects with artificial paintings or sculptures, fresh air with smoke, fresh water with pollutants, etc. The artificial life-style which technologism has created seeks to extend our legs with wheels, our brains with computers, our ears with radios, our eyes with pictures, etc. Therefore, technologism takes away the naturalness of man and the world. The prophecy of A. Huxley's Brave New World has become reality. The modern man who wants to have an authentic life-style needs to return to the natural life which authenticates his existence. The I Ching helps us to return to that natural way of life, for it is primarily based on the way of Nature. It is, in fact, the microcosm of it. As we have indicated, the Holy Sages surveyed the phenomena of nature and reduced them into hexagrams in the I Ching. Therefore, the eight trigrams, which are the bases for all hexagrams, represents the natural symbols: Heaven, Earth,

Wood, Wind, Water, Fire, Mountain and Lake. They are the simple and unadorned natural elements. Thus Change is the natural way which is characterized by the P'o (樸) or the virgin block of wood, the natural state of existence.[5] The natural way of life is spontaneous and free from constraint, but the artificial way of life is the slave of one's own life. The artificial way of life that is conventionally accepted cannot get away from what Herbert Marcuse calls "technological rationality." To overcome the artificial life-style is to break through the power of "technological rationality." It is the I Ching which frees us, for the I Ching conceives that chances, coincidences and spontaneities of the present are part of man's fullest reality. When the conventional life-style is overcome, we are restored to the original nature which alone gives our authentic existence.

Finally, the I Ching suggests that we must live as men of the cosmos, who are also ecological men. The men in the past have been interested in individualism and fought for their independence from the cosmos. The basic characteristic of Western man is the conquest of nature. Thus Braden says:

> Western man appears to be engaged in a kind of rape of
> mother Nature. And we all know that makes Western man,
> in the common parlance. One price he pays for this is
> alienation and isolation, the loss of cosmic connection:
> the feeling that he is at home in his own universe, not a
> cat burglar who has crept through a window to steal the
> silverware. He also pays another price: the loss of wonder.[6]

The ecological crisis that we face in our time was already latent in the idea of man to conquer nature. The idea that man is created to assert dominion over the earth has been the important creed not only for the development of scientific technology in the West but for man's alienation of himself from his own nature, the universe. Technology became the weapon to conquer nature, for the world was understood as his enemy. This dichotomy between man and nature must be eliminated, for man is the microcosm of the universe. We see more and more the dependence of man on the whole process of the universe. The ecological crisis in our time taught us that we are unable to separate ourselves from the ecosystem, which deals with the entire cosmos. The ecosystem is so delicate that the pollution of water, air, or soil will affect us directly. We are organically connected with the entire cosmos, so that what happens in the other side of the universe will eventually affect us.

The I Ching teaches us that we are part of the cosmic process of change, for we are microcosms of the universe. There is no dichotomy between man and the world. Man is the product of heaven and earth. This trinitarian view of the world became the key to the formation of trigrams and hexagrams in the I Ching. However insignificant we seem to be, we are replicas of the entire universe. We are, therefore, of the whole cosmos. It is the challenge of the I Ching that we must accept cosmic responsibility. Our life-style must be globally oriented. Henry

A. Kissinger, Secretary of the State, addressed the United Nations on

the necessity of building a global economy, which is the only solution

to an unjust world.[7] We need not only global economy but global politics,

global education, global love, etc., for we are global men. The new

life-style that we must adopt is then the holistic, complementary, and

unifying process of making the better world for all mankind.

CHAPTER X

THE I CHING AND THE MEANING OF DEATH

The idea of death is often misunderstood in the West. Death is known as the separation from life. In fact, death by definition often excludes life. In the world-affirming optimism which prevails in our time, death as the negation of life becomes the enemy of life. Death becomes not only undesirable but hostile, a force which must be destroyed. Because it is undesirable, it has been a forbidden topic in the past. As Price, Professor Emeritus at Cambridge University, said, "It is something worse. It is a topic which arouses such strong and uncomfortable emotions that we prefer not to mention it at all."[1] Even though death has become an important subject in academic study in recent times, the basic attitude of people toward death may not change unless we change their ways of thinking.

The misunderstanding of death as the enemy of life is largely attributed to the way of thinking in the past. As we have already indicated, we have inherited the exclusive way of thinking, which is fundamentally attributed to the Aristotelian logic of "either/or." Death is understood as an exclusion of life, just as life is known as an exclusion of death. Death cannot be included in life as long as we think in terms

of "either this or that." This kind of absolutistic thinking is, as we

have already pointed out, based on the dualistic world view, which is

rather superificial. In deeper reality things are in continuum, for they

are manifestations of Change. In the ultimate reality there is no

separation between opposites. Therefore, from the point of view of I

or Change in the I Ching death cannot be separated from life. The

exclusive way of thinking fails to function from the point of view of the

I Ching.

According to the I Ching life cannot be understood separately from

death. Since everything in the world can be reduced to the yin-yang

relationship, life and death are also known in terms of this relationship.

Just as yin is not possible without yang nor yang without yin, death is

unthinkable without life and life without death. They are mutually inclu-

sive and complementary. This relationship of yin and yang is a key to

the understanding of death and life together. Thus, "It is also said

there: 'If we investigate into the cycle of things (the cyclic relationship

or complementary relationship of yin and yang), we shall understand the

concept of life and death.'"[2] Just as the characteristics of yang and yin

are in apposition to each other, life and death are not identical but

inseparably related in their essence, which is change itself. As Tillich

said, "The conditions of death are the conditions of life."[3] A similar idea is evident in Tagore's philosophy: "Death and life are bound together by a single chain. The same chain binds those that are alive and those that are dead."[4] One fulfills the other. Tagore, who shares the root of Indian philosophy, seems to agree with the I Ching when he compares death with the bridegroom whose only bride is life:

> Why do you whisper so faintly in my ears,
> O Death, my Death?
> When the flowers droop in the evening and cattle come back
> to their stalls, you stealthily come to my side and speak
> words that I do not understand.
> Is this how you must woo and win me with the opiate or
> drowsy murmur and cold kisses,
> O Death, my Death?
> Will there be no proud ceremony of our wedding?
> Will you not tie up with a wreath your tawny coiled locks?
> Is there none to carry your banner before you, and will not
> the night be on fire with your red torchlights,
> O Death, my Death?
> Come with your conch-shells sounding, come in the sleep-
> less night.
> Dress me with a crimson mantle, grasp my hand and take me.
> Let your chariot be ready at my door with your horses neigh-
> ing impatiently.
> Raise my veil and look at my face proudly,
> O Death, my Death."[5]

Perhaps Tagore's most famous expression of death as the inseparable unity of life is expressed at his beloved wife's death.

> Dying, you have left behind you the great sadness of the
> Eternal in my life.
> You have painted my thought's horizon with the sunset
> colours of your departure, leaving a track of tears across
> the earth to love's heaven.
> Clasped in your dear arms, life and death united in me in
> a marriage bond.

I think I can see you watching there in the balcony with
your lamp lighted,
Where the end and the beginning of all things meet.
My world went hence through the doors that you opened--
You holding the cup of death to my lips, filling it with life
from your own.[6]

When death is regarded as the enemy of life, we fear of death and become

the victims of it.   But if we try to welcome death as the fulfillment of our

lives, we will be free from the fear.   The moment we accept death as our

own expression of life-force, we find it to be the gateway leading to a

fuller and richer life.

The inseparable unity of life and death is clearly expressed in the

diagram of the Great Ultimate, where yin and yang are mutually inter-

twined.   In the diagram we notice that yin or darkness is not absolutely

dark, because it contains a light dot.   On the other hand, yang or light

is not absolutely light, because it contains a dark dot.   Likewise, the

relationship between death and life is similar.   Just as there is the dot of

darkness in the light, so also there is the potential of death in life.   As

Tillich says, "Death is present in every life process from its beginning

to its end."[7] We can also say that death contains life, just as yin con-

tains yang.   Thus, Johnson says, "Death is to be explained in terms of

life.   It is a weak and indeed, insofar as it marks the final disintegra-

tion of one's nephesh, the weakest form of life; for it involves a complete

scattering of one's vital power."[8] Death is not the absolute extinction of life, but the minimum expression of it. On the other hand, life is not

the absolute exclusion of death, but the minimum presence of it. They

are mutually inherent to each other. Thus they are the manifestations of

the same source. As LeShan says, "The viewpoint that has seemed to

make the most sense to the writer is that life and death are both aspects

of the same _vital_ center, the same existence."[9] To separate one from

the other is to dismiss the possibility of our understanding both of them

together.

The inseparable relationship between life and death is clearly

expressed in the broken and unbroken symbols of yin and yang lines in

the _I Ching_. The broken line (— —) which signifies yin is none other

than the unbroken line (———) divided. On the other hand, the unbroken

line is none other than the broken line undivided. Both of them are two

different manifestations of one essence, the continuum of changing

process. They are essentially the same but existentially different. The

relationship between death and life is similar. Death is hidden or yin,

while life is manifested or yang in character. In other words, death is

life unmanifested, and life is death manifested. They are two sides of

one coin. Thus, Munro says, "'Life' and 'death' are human terms, and

are meaningless from the standpoint of eternity."[10] From the point of

view of Change, the ultimate reality, there is no clear distinction

between death and life. They are one stream of process, in which death and life come and go. "We live and die every moment of our lives. It is merely a coming into being and passing away like the waves of the sea."[11] They are none other than the phenomenal distinctions of one reality.

Since both death and life are manifestations of a single reality, death arises from life and life also comes from death. Lao Tzu seems to follow the same line of thinking:

> Death arises from life itself.
> For every three out of ten born
> Three out of ten die.
> But why in the face of death
> Should any three out of ten go on breeding,
> When all they produce is more death?
> Because of the wild obsession to multiply.
> But there is only one out of ten, so they say, so sure of life
> That the tiger and the wild bull avoid him in the hills
> And weapons turn from him on the field of war.
> The wild bull cannot find a place in him to pitch its horn,
> The tiger cannot find a place in which to dig its claws,
> The weapon's point can find no place in him to pierce.
> And why?
> Because when he dies he does not die.[12]

Just as the day is born out of night and night is possible because of the day, death arises from life, and life is found in death. Death is the background of life and life is the foreground of death. They are counterparts but never in conflict. They seem to follow certain orders of manifestation. Just as the moon appears when the sun is hidden, death arises when life is latent. When death becomes manifested, life withdraws itself within death. Since one arises from the other, there is no way to describe one without the other. They are best understood as a continuum.

In this kind of relationship death does not take away life. Rather, death is manifested out of life. Likewise, life never takes away death. Death is always with life. When death appears, life withdraws; when life appears, death withdraws also. Thus, one presupposes the existence of the other.

The co-existence of life and death can be illustrated through the use of hexagrams, which represent the archetypal situations of the universe. Even though each hexagram is autonomous, its autonomy is possible because of its relation to other hexagrams. Therefore, we must see each hexagram in light of every other hexagram. In order to illustrate the complementary existence of life and death, we can select twelve major hexagrams which will summarize the entire process of becoming. They begin with the first hexagram, Ch'ien and end up with the second hexagram, K'un. From these two primary hexagrams all other hexagrams come to exist. Since these hexagrams represent heaven and earth, they are the source of all other hexagrams in the I Ching. Life begins with the first hexagram and ends with the second. On the other hand, death begins with the second and ends with the first. If we take up the hexagrams between them, we come to notice the process of evolution from one end to the other. In other words, we may be able to see the patterns of evolvement from life to death and from death to life. The present life begins with the hexagram Ch'ien or Creativity and expands to the hexagrams <u>Kou</u>, <u>Tun</u>, <u>Fou</u>, <u>Kuan</u>, <u>Po</u>, and <u>K'un</u>, which marks the end of this life. On the other hand, the life after death begins with the hexagram <u>K'un</u> or Receptivity and expands to the hexagrams <u>Fu</u>, <u>Lin</u>, <u>T'ai</u>, <u>Ta Chuang</u>, <u>Kuai</u>, and <u>Ch'ien</u>, which marks the birth or rebirth of the dead.

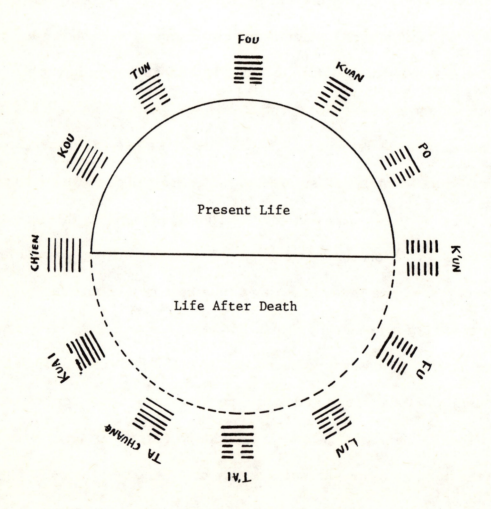

Let us first observe the changing process of the present life from the hexagram Ch'ien, which consists of yang lines only. All of the lines are unbroken. Thus it represents the infinite power of yang or creativity. It symbolizes the fullest expansion of the life-energy which takes place at the very moment of birth. It is the symbol of the dragon, which is the image of power and energy of infinite potential of growth. It corresponds to the fourth month, which means about May-June, the month before the summer. It represents the evolution of all things. The primary meaning of this hexagram is the creative becoming or the arousing of new life-power. Thus it is the creation of man as a new baby.

As soon as the baby is born at the hexagram Ch'ien, he starts to grow into youth, adulthood and old age. The first major stage of development of the present life is Kou (姤), which means Confrontation, the sudden confrontation of a yin element with yang forces. As we notice from the diagram, this hexagram consists of a yin or broken line in the beginning (or the below) and yang or unbroken lines above. Yin is the dark principle, which leads to decay and death. If we assume that the hexagram Kou represents the period of childhood, we notice that the dying process has already began. In other words, as soon as the baby was born at Ch'ien, which represents the pure life-force only, the death-power begins to expand in him. Thus, Conze says, "We start dying the moment we are born. The rate of metabolism in our bodies begins to slow down immediately after conception. Birth is the cause of death."[13] Here, we notice that the child confronts the power of decay or yin in the hexagram Kou. It is evident from this pattern of life and death that the process of growth is none other than the process of disintegration of life-forces. In other words, as soon as we are born the process of disintegration of life-energy begins and continues until death.

The next stage of the present life consists of the hexagram Tun (遯), which is made of two yin lines on the first and second places. Here, the increase of yin or the death-force is evident. This hexagram literally means Withdrawal or Retreat. From the composing primary trigrams we can easily notice that it is the symbol of withdrawal. The primary trigrams are the Creative or Ch'ien (☰) and the Stillness or Ken (☶). From the analysis of these trigrams we can notice that this hexagram means more than mere withdrawal. It really means creative non-action, which is often known as Wu-wei (無 爲) or non-doing in the philosophy of Taoism and the I Ching. This is the most creative period of life, because the power of creativity is not restricted by the external forces or the power of conventions. However, this creative power can only be exercised through quietness. The power of death increases in this hexagram, so that the most appropriate way to confront it is to be non-active. As Wilhelm comments, "The power of the dark is ascending. The light retreats to security, so that the dark cannot encroach upon it. This retreat is a matter not of man's will but of natural law."[14] Man cannot avoid the eventual increase of the power of death. The best way to deal with the power is to avoid the counter-action. As Jesus said, "But I say to you, do not resist one who is evil" (Matthew 5:39). Our resistance to the inevitable growth of yin power will aggravate it further. It is best not to react when dealing with the growing power of death.

The hexagram Fou or P'i (否) occupies the middle of the present life and means stagnation or a standstill. We notice that there are three yin lines below and three yang lines above; the powers of yin and yang are equal. It is now evident that the power of death is within the power of life. The life-power which is represented by the trigram Ch'ien (☰) is externalized, since it occupies the superior position. On the other hand, the death-power which is symbolized by the trigram K'un (☷) is internalized, for it occupies the inferior. Although the power of death occupies the center of one's life, the life-power is still active and he looks youthful from the outside. This hexagram represents middle age, youth suddenly becoming old. At this stage we often identify with youth but we find that we no longer have the vitality of youth. It corresponds to the seventh month, that is, about August-September, when the process of growth stops. Thus Legge says, "Genial influences have done their work, the processes of growth are at an end. Henceforth increasing decay must be looked for."[15]

The hexagram Kuan (觀) comes next. As we notice from the diagram, there are four yin lines in the interior and two yang lines in the exterior. The yin force definitely overweighs the yang force; the power of death fully dominates the power of life. The hexagram symbolizes old age and corresponds to the eighth month, that is, about September-October. It is the autumn season which is soon followed by winter, the season of death and complete decay. This hexagram means contemplation, which is part of the religious life and which is so important at this stage of aging. Thus the Judgment says, "The absolution has been performed, but not yet the offering." If we observe the constituting trigrams, they are K'un (☷) or earth below and Sun (☴) or wind above. Thus the image of this hexagram is: "The wind blows over the earth: the symbol of inner contemplation." Just as the wind over the earth blows off all external things, it symbolizes detachment from worldly desires and passions and allows one to contemplate his inner self. Detachment is essential for contemplation. This detachment is best represented by the end of the fall season when the leaves of the trees are dried and are blown off by the cold northern wind. It is, therefore, a lonely stage, preparing for the final decay.

The next hexagram is Po (剝), which means Peeling Off or Collapse. It is the symbol of the dying moment when the old is gradually drowned into the unconscious by the power of death. As we notice from the diagram, this hexagram consists of five yin lines with one yang line above, the single line retaining life. It corresponds to the very moment of death. "The dying is no longer in struggle but accepts the fact of dying as inevitable."[16] It seems to correspond to the last stage of death: Kübler-Ross says, "It is as if the pain had gone, the struggle is over, and there comes a time for 'the final rest before the long journey' as one patient phrased it."[17] It is said, "He faces the end of normal life process and looks for a sign."[18] The sign that the dying man looks for is known as the Great Light which appears at the very moment of total disintegration of self. The Great Light is the sign that must be realized by the dying if he is going to be liberated from the chain of karma. As the representation of this hexagram indicates, it consists of Ken (☶) or mountain and K'un (☷) or earth. It means the mountain resting on the earth. It is, then, the image of peace and tranquility in spite of the imminent disintegration of the whole self. This image of steadiness and tranquility depicts well the last state of the dying person. There is a sense of calmness and serenity in the last moment of death. This hexagram corresponds to October-November, the cold winter season, the season of dying and death.

Finally, the total disintegration of the body takes place at the hexagram K'un (坤) or the earth. The body which belongs to the earth will return to earth when it is totally disintegrated. Thus the hexagram of earth is the last symbol, completing the cycle of life. The life-power is totally extinguished by the death-power. Thus in the hexagram there is no yang line. The conscious self is completely disintegrated and the unconscious is totally revealed. According to the Bardo Thödol or the Tibetan Book of the Dead, this moment of total disintegration is known as Chikhai Bardo, which is the state of "swoon." Those who have practiced yoga can realize the coming of the Clear Light of the Void and be enlightened.[19] It is in the deepest abyss of one's own self. It is the symbol of total attachment to the world, which is possibly only through the total detachment from the world. This paradoxical identity between the total attachment and detachment is possible because the hexagram K'un presupposes the existence of the hexagram Ch'ien. Just as yin principle presupposes the yang principle, K'un, the primordial principle of yin, cannot exist without its counterpart, Ch'ien, the primordial principle of yang. Since the hexagram Ch'ien, the primordial principle of life, is the background of the hexagram K'un, the primordial principle of death, the former grows as soon as man dies. In other words, the yang principle begins to appear as soon as yang principle reaches its maximum. Thus the hexagram K'un is followed by the hexagram Fu or Returning, which starts a new cycle of the rebirth process.

As we have pointed out, the present life cycle begins with the hexagram Ch'ien and ends with the hexagram K'un, while the cycle of life after death begins with the hexagram K'un and ends with the hexagram Ch'ien. In this respect, the beginning of life-after-death is the end of life-before-death. Since the end and beginning are identical, everything is in the cyclic process of becoming. Thus Govinda said, "There is not one person, indeed, not one living being, that has not returned from death. In fact, we all have died many deaths, before we came into this incarnation."[20] If death and life are in a cyclic pattern, it is valuable to study the cycle which begins with death and ends with birth. This cycle, then, deals with the life after death or the Bardo phenomena.

Just as the decay of the life-power begins with birth, the decay of the power of death begins with death. As soon as one dies, he starts to live. In other words, at the moment of death the life-process begins. Thus the hexagram K'un is followed by the hexagram Fu (復) or Returning, signifying a return to life. It is the counterpart of the hexagram Kou, which deals with the confrontation of the death-power. Here in the hexagram Fu new life begins to return to the dead. Thus it is the recovery of consciousness. It is also the recovery of the dead from the "swoon," the state of total unconsciousness. As we notice from the diagram, the yang principle or life appears at the first place or at the bottom of the hexagram. Because of this, the dead is conscious of his own death and begins to experience the reality of death. "Thus with this hexagram the dead is ushered into the Chönyid Bardo or the inter-mediate state of experiencing the reality of death."[21] According to the Tibetan Book of the Dead, Karmic impressions begin to appear in this intermediate state. Furthermore, the dead can visualize his own death and notice the relatives and friends who are weeping for him:

> About this time the deceased can see that the share of food
> is being set aside, that the body is being stripped of its
> garments, that the place of the sleeping-rug is being swept;
> can hear all the weeping and wailing of his friends and
> relatives, and although he can see them and can hear them
> calling upon him, they cannot hear him calling upon them,
> so he goeth away displeased.[22]

As the symbol of this hexagram indicates, it is similar to the thunder within the earth, the emergence of new life within the soil. It is the beginning of new life, of reincarnation.

The life-principle grows in the hexagram Lin (臨), which means "Approach." In this hexagram yang lines occupy both the first and second places and the rest are yin lines. This is the counterpart of the hexagram Tun or withdrawal. While in Tun the passive action is required to maintain the creative process, in Lin the active approach is needed to move forward the process of new becoming. As we notice from the diagram, the hexagram <u>Lin</u> consists of <u>Tui</u> (☱) or a body of water and <u>K'un</u> (☷) or the earth. It means the water within the earth. <u>Tui</u> as the body of water is also the most youthful daughter who is the symbol of vitality. Therefore, the hexagram signifies that the reserved water approaches or moves upward to break through the ground. This is then the time of growth and expansion of the consciousness of the dead. This expansion of life-power within the after-death state is so active that it cannot be prevented. According to the <u>Bardo Thödol</u>, the dead at this stage expands the vision of his <u>karmic</u> impressions. He begins to see various visions which are none other than his own thought-forms. It is followed by the hexagram <u>T'ai</u>.

   <u>T'ai</u> (泰) literally means "peace," which is the counterpart of <u>Fou</u> or stagnation. <u>T'ai</u> is a symbol of perfect harmony between the life and death principles. As we see from the diagram, it consists of <u>K'un</u> (☷) or earth above and <u>Ch'ien</u> (☰) or heaven below. Since <u>K'un</u> is a heavy principle, it tends to come down. On the other hand, the <u>Ch'ien</u> is a light principle that tends to go up. Therefore, they meet each other to produce all things. It is the symbol of perfect union of both male and female that engenders many offspring. Thus at this inter- mediate state the dead can see many visions of peaceful deities with various colors of radiance from all directions.[23] At this hexagram the

dead not only enjoys the colorful cinema of his own images, but is also terrified with it.

The hexagram Ta Chuang (大 壯) comes next. As soon as the dead passes T'ai, he enters into the Sidpa Bardo or the intermediate state of rebirth. Even though rebirth begins as soon as the dead recovers from the deep "swoon," the actual process of rebirth is more intensely realized in this period, which marks the end of the intermediate state. As we notice from the hexagram, it consists of four yang lines below and two yin lines above. The vital life-energy is certainly dominating the power of death. The life power from below surges upward for reincarnation. Because these life principles are so powerful, the name of this hexagram is "The Power of the Great" or Ta Chuang. This great power is accompanied with the character of arousing. As the constituting trigrams consist of Ch'ien (☰) or heaven and Chen (☳) or Arousing, the great life power is aroused for reincarnation. It corresponds to the second month, that is, March-April. It is the Spring time when the seeds start to sprout and the germination of the dead begins. The hexagram Ta Chuang is, then, the symbol of great attachment to life, while the hexagram Kuan or contemplation, which is the counterpart of Ta Chuang, is the symbol of great detachment from earthly passions. The former stresses self-assertion, while the latter is interested in non-assertion of self.

The hexagram Kuai (夬) means Resolution or Break-Through, which is the counterpart of the hexagram Po or Collapse. The former means "a break-through after a long accumulation of tension, as a swollen river breaks through its dikes, or in the manner of a cloudburst."[24] When it is applied to the rebirth process, it means the opening of the womb for the actual birth process. Just as the hexagram Po depicts the very moment of dying, the hexagram Kuai describes the very moment of rebirth. The latter corresponds to the third month of April-May, at which time the germinated seeds start to burst out from the ground. Kuai consists of one yin line at the top and five yang lines below. The life-principle almost completely overcomes the death-principle. From the constituting trigrams we notice that the upper one is Tui (☱) or joy and the lower trigram is Ch'ien (☰) or creativity. Thus it means the joy over the creative process of childbirth.

This joy is completed in the hexagram Ch'ien (乾) or the Creative. The rebirth process is finished and the yang principle completely dominates the hexagram. It is the perfect expansion of the vital life-energy, which complements the hexagram K'un, which expresses the perfect expansion of the passive death-power. The hexagram Ch'ien symbolizes the dragon, which has the infinite source of vital energy and creativity. This is the month corresponding to May-June, at which time things start to grow in full. This is also similar to noon, the zenith of the sun. The light principle starts to decay as soon as it reaches the zenith, death or decay begins as soon as life is manifest. Ch'ien is then the beginning of new life as well as the end of the old life, the life of previous birth. Thus another cycle of life and death begins again.

With the use of hexagrams, we have determined that life and death are mutually complementary. Life is the underside of death and death is the underside of life. They are counterparts that fulfill the whole. Life without death is meaningless, only a partial expression of human existence. Thus death actually fulfills life and makes life meaningful. Therefore, from the point of view of the I Ching, death and life are only different manifestations of a single reality, which is the Change that changes all things. To be in that Change means to transcend our existence from the cycle of birth and death. That is the Liberation, which is the ultimate goal of human destiny.

CHAPTER XI

CONCLUSION WITH ISSUES AND PROBLEMS

From previous essays we cannot overestimate the fact that the
I Ching is more than an historical and cultural expression of certain situations. The I Ching seems to transcend time and space, having perennial
significance to all men and all situations. It can be regarded as the col-
lection of archetypes which are the roots of all civilizations. The 64
hexagrams in the I Ching should be understood as the major archetypes
of everything that was, is and will be. However highly cultured people
we might be, we are still conditioned by archetypes. Progression and
retrogression are none other than temporary manifestions of the same
reality, which may be compared to the waves of the sea. They come and
go, but the essential reality of water does not change. The I Ching, then,
contains the archetypes which close the gap between the archaic people
and the modern men as well as the Far Eastern countries and the Western
nations. Therefore, we see the relevance of the I Ching in every walk of
our lives.

The conviction that the I Ching contains the archetypes of the
universe is derived from a long history of experiments on the I Ching

rather than from any logical or rational proof of its validity. Carl G. Jung

in the West seems to voice a similar conviction when he accepts the

work of the I Ching on the basis of his experience.[1] Those who have

enough faith to experiment with the I Ching seem to be convinced that it

really works. They do not have much trouble accepting that the I Ching

contains the basic archetypes which can be applicable to all situations

in life. However, for those who base their judgments on the conventional

and rational frames of reference the hexagrams in the I Ching are mean-

ingless arrangements of broken and unbroken lines. For them these

arrangements signify a mere mathematical game. If the I Ching happens

to correspond to the mentality of the contemporary man, it must be

regarded as purely coincidental. Tough-minded skeptics who disbelieve

in the I Ching ask the question: "Isn't it a pure coincidence that the

idea of change in the I Ching happens to be compatible with those aspects

of modern man that this book has attempted to describe?" This is an

important question if this book is to stand on its own, since it is written

to the audience whose experience does not extend enough to be convinced

by the authenticity of the I Ching.

One of our first reactions to this question is "yes." Yes, it is

possible that basic ideas in the I Ching happen to coincide with some of

the pertinent thoughts of modern man. It can be a pure coincidence that,

for example, the development of modern science is compatible with the basic metaphysical system of the I Ching. Let us begin our discussion with the assumption that it is a pure accident that the ideas of the I Ching and those of modern man are closely related. Unless we give meaning to this idea of "pure coincidence," we cannot expect skeptics to see the value of the I Ching in their lives.

The idea of coincidence is a key to the I Ching. It is a means to the understanding of reality. It is in fact a counterpart of our causality process. Coincidence is a meaningful connection by chance. Because it is based on chance rather than the cause-effect principle, it is often known as an acausal connection over against the causal connection. These are not in contradiction to each other. They are mutually comple- mentary. One cannot exist without the other. When the causality prin- ciple dominates the world, the world is seen as a big machine. When the acausality principle dominates the world, the world becomes chaos. Both are essential aspects of a free and ordered world. Even most primitive religions have accepted this kind of world view, where both cause and chance are mutually correlated. Thus Max Born rightly points out the inevit- able co-existence of both causality and acausality principles in nature:

> In fact, all primitive polytheistic religions seem to be based on such a conception of nature: things happening in haphazard way, except where some spirit interferes with a purpose. We reject to-day this demonological philosophy, but admit chance into the realm of exact science. Our philosophy is dualistic in this respect; nature is ruled by the laws of cause and laws of chance in a certain mixture.[2]

Nature as well as human affairs are subject to both necessity and accident, for they are complementary to each other. We cannot say that one is valid and the other is not, for one cannot exist without the other. Their relation is similar to the yin and yang relationship. Just as yin is true because of yang and yang because of yin, necessity is meaningful because of accident and accident is meaningful because of necessity. If there is a law of causality in the world, there must be the law of chance also. What we think of as mere coincidence is not without meaning. It seems to be meaningless to us because we cannot coin it in our rational and logical frame of reference which seems to make a meaningful connection to the limited mind. If meaning is derived from our limited understanding of the causality principle alone, this meaning is not really meaningful at all. On the other hand, coincidence is meaningless from the point of view of the causality principle, but it is meaningful when it is considered from the point of view of acausality. Since "nature is ruled by the laws of cause and laws of chance in a certain mixture,"[3] it is difficult to say that causal connections are only meaningful and chance connections or acausal connections are meaningless. Therefore, we must say that there is neither "pure chance" nor "pure cause" in the world. Chance is always co-existing with cause, for they are relative to each other.

Let us illustrate the idea of coincidence. For example, it is arbitrary or coincidental to connect the symbol of the cross with Christ for those who have never heard of Christ. However, for those who are Christians it is meaningful because they can recognize its connection on the basis of their limited frame of reference. We have used a lottery system to draft young people into military service in the past. It is based on a chance operation. Is it meaningless to a young man who happens to have a chosen number? Is it meaningless to win or to lose the game which is based on chance? Is it meaningless to meet someone whom we have never expected? We must say that their connections are as meaningful as the causal connections in reality. The coincidental connections or connections by chance seem to be meaningless because the meaning is hidden in them. The hidden meaning eventually manifests itself in our experience. It seems to be a mere coincidence for most skeptics to see the connection of the I Ching with modern man. However, this coincidence is full of meaning which is latent in their experiences. For those who have recognized the profundity of the I Ching the meaning is manifest in their lives.

The latent meaning in coincidence cannot be revealed to us unless it is integrated in our experience. It cannot be rationalized or placed in the frame of our logical reference. The intrinsic meaning which is inherent in coincidence or chance cannot be structured by our rational system.

Whenever we attempt to place it in our rational frame of reference, it loses authenticity. It can be experienced only, because experience deals with the totality of existence. Carl Jung attempts to define the hidden meaning of coincidence through his theory of "synchronicity," which was later defended by Arthur Koestler.[4] Synchronicity rejects the idea of pure or mere chance theory. As we have already pointed out, there is no pure chance or pure cause, since they are mutually complementary. Just as yin is not pure in itself but always part of yang and yang is not completely yang but always part of yin, chance is not pure random but always part of cause. Therefore, synchronicity rejects the theory that events coincide as meaningless. Carl Jung suggested from a study of horoscopes that the correlation of the positions of the horoscopes among married people is more than a mere chance. He concluded, "Their concurrence, however, is so improbable that one cannot help assuming the existence of an impelling factor that produced this result."[5] There is also a surprising result of coincidence between the psychic condition of the questioner and the answering hexagram in the I Ching. There is reliability and certain order behind the coincidental principle that is not revealed in our ordinary or conventional process of thinking. This hidden order and consistency seems to appear through a medium of hexagrams or horoscopes. Therefore, Carl Jung said, "The I Ching presupposes that there is a synchronistic correspondence between the psychic state of the questioner and the answering hexagram."[6] In other words, the divination process is one means to reveal the hidden meaning of coincidence.

Synchronicity or the acausal connecting principle reveals meaning in many different ways. If it deals with the meaningful correlation of the visible and invisible or of the spiritual and material, it does not come under the domain of scientific investigation, but is experienced in various activities which are unconventional. We see the evidence of synchronic correlation in the shamanistic dance, for example, where the shaman acts spontaneously according to the spirit. The most clear evidence of this kind is found in the event of Pentecost in the Acts of Apostles in the New Testament. Speaking with tongues implies the movement of tongues according to the spirit. Here, the meaningful correlation between the tongues and spiritual activities is evident. Spiritual healing, for example, is another illustration of the acausal connection between the material and the spiritual realms. They coincide with each other but their coincidence is more than _mere_ chance. In the same manner the symbols of the hexagrams can become a most effective means of revealing the hidden meaning of coincidence. Thus the divination process of the _I Ching_ belongs to the unconventional or unorthodox way of seeing meaning in chance operations.

Because of its lack of convention, the divination of the I Ching, like all other forms of divination, has been subject to the suspicion of the public. This negative attitude towards divination is due to the misunderstanding of its profundity. Divination is not superstitious. It does not deal with something that is unreal, with the partial world which we have created through the use of causality principle alone; rather it deals with what is more real to our experience as a whole. Since divination attempts to deal with our unconsciousness which does not reveal directly to our conscious mind, its function must be different from scientific discipline, which deals with the realm of the conscious only. Since the strata of both the conscious and the unconscious are mutually inclusive and interdependent, both divination and technical science must be complementary rather than dichotomous to each other. Sound civilization seems to allow both to co-exist for the fulfillment of the spiritual and material welfare of the people.

Divination ought not to be accused of being heretical. The right use of divination does not go against the Christian faith. If we have the right to investigate the empirical world through natural science, we also have the same right to investigate the unconscious world through the divination process. Just as science is not the enemy of religion, divination cannot be either. Rather, both of them belong to the domain of religion if religion is concerned with the totality of human existence.

Unless we change our attitude toward the divination process, the I Ching cannot be fully appreciated in our time.

Another problem closely connected with divination is fatalism. If divination deals with the fatalistic determinism of human destiny, it goes against human creativity and freedom, which are indispensable to our value system. Fatalism is closely related with the idea of wish, which is a mere expection regardless of responsibility. Just like the idea of wish, fatalism is an enemy of human autonomy and a seed of irresponsible society. Consequently, any form of divination which is based on fatalism cannot be effective. The I Ching has been active in the main stream of Far Eastern civilization because it could overcome the power of fatalistic determinism. The I Ching, unlike many other divination books, denies fatalism. The primary purpose of consulting this book is not to accept fate blindly but to control it. While fatalism is associated with wish, the I Ching is closely associated with hope. Hope is different from wish, because it is based on the concrete experience of present reality. The I Ching can give us promises or germinal situations that direct our hope toward actual realization. Because of this hope, freedom is allowed in the I Ching. As we have already pointed out in Chapter VIII, the I Ching allows limited freedom, which seems to be more practical and sound than the illusory notion of unlimited freedom. Freedom is relative to the hexa-gram or germination situation in which we find our own existence. Real freedom is, according to the I Ching, the freedom of actualization. Let

us take up the hexagram six, Sung (訟) or Conflict. In Legge's trans-

lation the Judgment on this hexagram says:

> Sung intimates how, though there is sincerity in one's con-
> tention, he will yet meet with opposition and obstruction;
> but if he cherish an apprehensive caution, there will be good
> fortune, while, if he must prosecute the contention to the
> (bitter) end, there will be evil. It will be advantageous to
> see the great man; it will not be advantageous to cross the
> great stream.

The Judgment is neither deterministic nor fatalistic but instructional.

Because of its instructional nature, it allows relative freedom, which is

neither the denial of freedom nor the denial of responsibility. Relative

freedom implies the relative determinism in the I Ching. This kind of

freedom is more realistic than the unlimited freedom that we often think

we have.

Even though a text is instructional in nature, it is in most cases so

ambiguous that all kinds of interpretation can be made. In other words,

no matter what hexagrams are selected through the divination process,

it is possible to interpret them so as to apply to any question the

questioner asks. There is no specific and concrete instruction; the text

is only interested in a probable trend. There is enough room for creative

and intuitive interpretations of the hexagram, even though its disadvantage

is the lack of precise guidelines. It is self-defeating to receive the ser-

vice of professional diviners. The real value of the ambiguous texts in

the I Ching is to provide a chance to bring out our personal interpretations through the projection of our unconsciousness. However, those
who are interested in the scholarly study of the I Ching must face
hermeneutic problems, the problems of interpretation.

The hermeneutic question arises in almost all forms of academic
study in classical literature. This question is more serious to our study
of the I Ching, because it is primarily a book of symbols and oracles.
Unlike other books, the I Ching presents two distinctive forms of
symbolism: symbolism without words, and symbolism with words. The
former or more primary is represented by hexagrams or lineal symbols,
and the latter in judgments. Because of the opaqueness of the symbols
in the I Ching, it has been regarded as one of the most difficult books to
understand. Even though the I Ching has been one of the most popular
books in our time, only a limited number of people are genuinely interested
in pursuing the academic study of this book.

In order to interpret the primary symbols or hexagrams, we have to
have some background in the basic metaphysics and cosmology of the
I Ching. Without this foundation, it is almost impossible to understand
the significance of the hexagrams. Each hexagram must be seen in light
of the entire pattern of changing process. There is no way to understand
it in separation from the whole. Each line in the hexagram must be understood in relation to the hexagram as a whole. Thus everything is

interdependent. Moreover, it necessitates creative imaginations and insights to entertain the abstract symbol of lines. Without such insights, the study of hexagrams is not possible. If we are interested in the rational or conventional approach to hexagrams, we will never succeed. It is unusually difficult to study the I Ching as an academic discipline. On the other hand, it is a real challenge to take up the study of the I Ching in the academic community, because it is not only innovative but allows deep insights into the mystery of our unconscious world.

The interpretation of the secondary symbols or judgments is also difficult because of their inconsistencies. In most cases the judgments are interpreted according to the attributes of the constituting trigrams. However, there are many exceptions to this rule. Often the judgments are based on the structure of the hexagram itself. When the hexagram resembles an observation tower, as, for example, the hexagram Kuan (觀), the judgment is decided by the structure. Thus it is named as "Contemplation" or "View." In many other cases we cannot find any unifying rationale for the ascription of a certain name to the hexagrams. There are no definite guidelines for the interpretation of symbols in the I Ching. To the unenlightened and conventional mind the I Ching seems to be irrational and arbitrary. Nevertheless, for those who are aware with new insights and higher forms of wisdom, it is certainly a master-piece that outweighs all other books.

In addition to these difficulties, we must learn how to live and to think according to the teaching of the I Ching. In it are the beauties of simplicity, a straight and uncontaminated life. To be a student of the I Ching means to be more than a thinking person. One must be a practicing person. When we are entangled with many conflicts and dichotomies, the I Ching shows us the way to freedom. We should learn that conflicts are not real but superficial. We must learn how to live a simple life within a complex society, how to live purely and naturally within a polluted and artificial world. The I Ching also teaches us the life of a whole person. We are not bits of the whole but we are the whole. Whatever is found in the universe is also found within us. We are the entirety, for we are microcosms of the complete world. Even though we have made amazing technological and cultural advancements, there are still many insights that the I Ching can teach us if we are open to its wisdom.

FOOTNOTES

Chapter I

[1]One of the typical examples is found in The Richard Wilhelm's Translation, published by Princeton University Press, 1967.

[2]Chapter 1.

[3]Section I, Chapter 2.

[4]Li Chi, VII, 2.

[5]Shih Ching, II, ii. 18.

[6]Ibid., V, iv. 20, 31.

[7]Fung Yu-lan, A History of Chinese Philosophy, Vol. I (Princeton: Princeton University Press, 1952), p. 380.

[8]Analects, IX. 8.

[9]Li Chi, VIII. 4.

[10]Ta Chuan, Sec. I, Ch. 11.

[11]Chu Shun-sheng, Liu-shih-ssu Kua ching chieh (朱駿聲 六十四卦經解), Peking, 1958, p. 2.

[12]Ta Chuan, Sec. II, Ch. 11.

[13]For comprehensive treatise on the origin and formation of the I Ching, see author's The Principle of Changes: Understanding the I Ching (Secaucus, N.J.: University Books, 1971), pp. 14ff.; Author's "Some Reflections on the Authorship of the I Ching" in Numen, Vol. XVII, Fasc. 3 (December 1970), pp. 200-210.

[14]For comprehensive treatise on the origin of the Ten Wings, see author's *The Principle of Changes: Understanding the I Ching*, pp. 28ff.

[15]H. G. Creel, *Confucius and the Chinese Way* (New York: Harper and Row, 1960), p. 199.

[16]*Ibid.*

[17]*Analects*, XIII. 22.

[18]*Ibid.*, VII. 16.

[19]H. G. Creel, *op. cit.*, p. 105; Fung Yu-lan, *op. cit.*, pp. 381f.

[20]*Analects*, VII. 5.

Chapter II

[1]*The Principle of Changes*, p. 5.

[2]*Ta Chuan*, Sec. II, Ch. 5.

[3]*Ibid.*, Sec. I, Ch. 5.

[4]*The Principle of Changes*, p. 59.

[5]*Ta Chuan*, Sec. I, Ch. 1.

[6]*Tao Te Ching*, Ch. 16 (Chang Chung-yuan's translation).

[7]Chang Chung-yuan, *Creativity and Taoism* (New York: Harper and Row, 1970), p. 127.

[8]*T'uan Chuan*, Sec. II, Hex. 32.

[9]*Ibid.*, Sec. I, Hex. 16, Line 3 (James Legge's translation).

[10]*Analects*, IX. 16.

[11]*Ta Chuan*, Sec. I, Ch. 5.

[12]Ch'eng I, _Erh-Ch'eng I-shu_ (二 程 遺 書), XV. 7b.

[13]Josiah Royce, _Lectures on Modern Idealism_ (New Haven: Yale University Press, 1919), p. 96.

[14]Chang Tsai, _Collected Works_, Book II, Sec. I.

[15]_I Ching: Book of Changes_, Translated by James Legge, Edited by Ch'u Chai with Winberg Chai (New Hyde Park, New York: University Books, 1964), p. 55.

[16]See _The Principle of Changes_, p. 106.

[17]Chang Chung-yuan, _op. cit._, p. 9.

[18]_Ta Chuan_, Sec. I, Ch. 11.

[19]_Shuo Kua_ 11.

[20]_Ta Chuan_, Sec. I, Ch. 4.

[21]_Ibid_.

Chapter III

[1]Carl G. Jung, "In Memory of Richard Wilhelm," in _The Secret of the Golden Flower_, tr. by Richard Wilhelm (New York: Harcourt, Brace and World, 1962), p. 141.

[2]Carl G. Jung, "Commentary," in _The Secret of the Golden Flower_, p. 82.

[3]Carl G. Jung, "Foreword," in _The I Ching or Book of Changes_, tr. by Richard Wilhelm and C. F. Baynes (Princeton: Princeton University Press, 1967), p. xxiv.

[4]_The Secret of the Golden Flower_, p. 141.

[5]Paul Veide, "Poor Man's Computer," in _Commonwealth_, March 8, 1968, p. 693.

[6]The Secret of the Golden Flower, p. 142.

[7]Ibid.

[8]Ibid., p. 81.

[9]Wilfred C. Smith, The Faith of Other Men (New York: New American Library of World Literature, 1963), p. 77.

[10]Jean Gebser, "The Trend Towards Integration in Modern Science and Its Counterpart in the Ancient Wisdom of the East," in Eastern Wisdom and Western Thought, by P. J. Saher (London: George Allen and Unwin, 1969), p. 10.

[11]Ibid.

[12]Arthur Koestler, The Roots of Coincidence (New York: Random House, 1972), p. 67.

[13]Sheila Ostrander and Lynn Schroeder, Psychic Discoveries Behind the Iron Curtain (Englewood Cliffs, N. J.: Prentice-Hall, 1970), p. 213.

[14]Cf. Author's The I (New York: Philosophical Library, 1971), pp. 4-11; "Yin-Yang Way of Thinking," in International Review of Mission, Vol. LX, No. 239, pp. 363-370.

[15]Sec. I, Ch. 11.

[16]Ta Chuan, Sec. I, Ch. 5: This is a literal translation of "一陰一陽之謂道." See author's The Principle of Changes: Understanding the I Ching (New Hyde Park: University Books, 1971), p. 74.

[17]Ch'u Chai with Winberg Chai, "Introduction," in I Ching, tr. by James Legge (Secaucus, N.J.: University Books, 1964), pp. xl-xli.

[18]Cf. The Principle of Changes, pp. 141ff.

[19]The Secret of the Golden Flower, p. 82.

[20]Ta Chuan, Sec. I, Ch. 8.

[21]*Tao Te Ching*, Ch. 2.

[22]*The Secret of the Golden Flower*, p. 141.

Chapter IV

[1]Hellmut Wilhelm, *Change: Eight Lectures on the I Ching* (New York: Harper and Row, 1960), p. 3.

[2]Wilfred Cantwell Smith, *The Faith of Other Men* (New York: The New American Library, 1963), p. 67.

[3]Joseph Needham, *Science and Civilization in China*, Vol. II (Cambridge: At the University Press, 1969), p. 498.

[4]*Ibid.*, p. 505.

[5]See author's *Principle of Changes: Understanding the I Ching* (Secaucus, N.J.: University Books, 1971), pp. 45-52.

[6]*Ibid.*, p. 277.

[7]William Bonner, *The Mystery of the Expanding Universe* (New York: Macmillan Co., 1964), p. 90.

[8]James A. Coleman, *Relativity for the Laymen* (New York: William-Frederick Press, 1958), p. 41.

[9]Max Born, *Natural Philosophy of Causes and Chance* (New York: Dover Publications, 1964), p. 3.

[10]Werner Heisenberg, *Physics and Beyond: Encounter and Conversations* (New York: Harper and Row, 1971), p. 113.

[11]Arthur S. Eddington, "The Decline of Determinism" in *Great Essays in Science*, ed. by Martin Gardner (New York: Washington Square Press, 1961), p. 254.

[12]*Ibid.*, p. 253.

[13]W. Heisenberg, *op. cit.*, p. 81.

[14]Arthur Koestler, The Roots of Coincidence (New York: Random House, 1972), p. 51.

[15]According to the Uncertainty Principle of Quantum Mechanics, the product of the uncertainties in the measured values of the position and momentum (i.e., the product of mass and velocity) cannot be smaller than Planck's constant. See W. Heisenberg, op. cit., p. 78.

[16]Ibid., p. 104.

[17]Ta Chuan, Sec. I, Ch. 5.

[18]W. Heisenberg, op. cit., p. 105.

[19]Carl G. Jung, Structure and Dynamics of the Psyche, Collected Works, Vol. VIII. Tr. by R. F. C. Hull (London, 1960), p. 318.

[20]W. Heisenberg, op. cit., p. 163.

[21]Werner Heisenberg, Philosophic Problems of Nuclear Science (New York: Pantheon Books, 1952), p. 15.

[22]Quoted by Koestler, op. cit., p. 54.

[23]W. Heisenberg, Physics and Beyond, pp. 84-85.

[24]Ibid., p. 79.

[25]See James D. Watson, The Double Helix: A Personal Account of the Discovery of the Structure of DNA (New York: Atheneum Publishers, 1968).

[26]Ta Chuan, Sec. II, Ch. 5.

[27]G. Gamow, Mr. Tompkings in Paperback (Cambridge: At the University Press, 1967), p. 136.

[28]Kenneth Ford, The World of Elementary Particles (London: Blaisdell, 1963), p. 168.

[29]The value numbers deal with the actual process of divination. See author's The Principle of Changes, pp. 248ff.

[30]Martin Gardner, "Mathematical Games: The Combinational Basis of the 'I Ching,' the Chinese Book of Divination and Wisdom," in Scientific American, January, 1974, p. 110.

[31]Hellmut Wilhelm, "Leibniz and the I-Ching," in Collectonea Commissionis Synodalis (Peking), 1943, p. 215.

[32]Veide, Commonwealth, p. 693.

[33]W. Heisenberg, Physics and Beyond, p. 41.

[34]A. Koestler, op. cit., p. 61.

Chapter V

[1]See his "I Have Seen Acupuncture Work," in Today's Health, July 1972 (Vol. 50, No. 7), pp. 50ff.

[2]See the article, "Acupuncture U.S. Style," in Newsweek, June 12, 1972, p. 74.

[3]Eileen Simpson, "Acupuncture," in Saturday Review, February 19, 1972, p. 49.

[4]Eric Utne, "Acupuncture in America," in East/West Journal, September 1973 (Vol. 3, No. 9), p. 14.

[5]Complete Works of Lu Hsiang-shan, Vol. XXXIII; Quoted in Chang Chung-yuan, Creativity and Taoism: A Study of Chinese Philosophy, Art, and Poetry (New York: The Julian Press, 1963), p. 82.

[6]Ibid.

[7]Arnold Toynbee, Man's Concern with Death (New York: McGraw-Hill, 1968), pp. 180-181.

[8]Ta Chuan, Sec. I, Ch. 8.

[9]Ch'ien Han Shu (前漢書), Ch. 81; Quoted in Fung Yu-lan, A History of Chinese Philosophy, Vol. II, tr. by Derk Bodde (Princeton: Princeton University Press, 1953), p. 20.

[10]See Fung Yu-lan, _op_. _cit_., p. 97.

[11]Carsun Chang, The Development of Neo-Confucian Thought (New York: Boodman Associates, 1962), p. 172.

[12]Marc Duke, Acupuncture (New York: Pyramid House, 1972), pp. 102ff.

Chapter VI

[1]Josef Rudin, Psychotherapy and Religion, tr. by Elisabeth Reinecke and Paul C. Bailey (Notre Dame: University of Notre Dame Press, 1968), p. 127.

[2]Edward C. Whitmont, The Symbolic Quest: Basic Concepts of Analytical Psychology (New York: C. G. Jung Foundation for Analytical Psychology, 1969), p. 178.

[3]Ibid.

[4]Erich Fromm, "Psychoanalysis and Zen Buddhism," in Zen Buddhism and Psychoanalysis, ed. by D. T. Suzuki, Erich Fromm, and Richard De Martino (New York: Harper and Row, 1960), p. 126.

[5]Ibid., p. 96.

[6]Rudin, _op_. _cit_., p. 130.

[7]Ibid., p. 61.

[8]Ibid., p. 127.

[9]Carl G. Jung, The Collected Works of C. G. Jung (New York: Pantheon Books), IX, pp, 1, 4; VII, p. 136.

[10]Josef Goldbrunner, Individuation: A Study of the Depth Psychology of Carl Gustav Jung (Notre Dame: University of Notre Dame, 1964), p. 105.

[11]Ibid., p. 116.

[12]Ibid., p. 108.

[13]For the detailed information on the process of divination see author's The Principle of Changes: Understanding the I Ching (Secaucus, N.J.: University Books, 1971), pp. 239-273.

[14]Carl G. Jung, "Foreword," The I Ching or Book of Changes: The Richard Wilhelm Translation, Third Edition (Princeton: Princeton University Press, 1969), p. xxxix.

Chapter VII

[1]Thomas Aquinas, Summa Theologica (New York: McGraw-Hill, n.d.), Ia. 9, 3.

[2]See The Holy Bible: Revised Standard Version Containing Old and New Testaments (New York: Thomas Nelson and Sons, 1952), p. 58, footnote.

[3]This last translation may be closest to the original meaning of the text, and is discussed in greater detail elsewhere in this article.

[4]See John Courtney Murray, The Problem of God: Yesterday and Today (New Haven: Yale University Press, 1964), p. 7.

[5]Edmond Jacob, Theology of the Old Testament, tr. by Arthur W. Heathcote and Philip J. Allcock (New York: Harper and Brothers, 1958), p. 54.

[6]Paul Tillich, Systematic Theology (Chicago: University of Chicago Press, 1951), I, 238.

[7]Kena 3.

[8]Katha 6:12.

[9]See the argument in Edward Conze, Buddhism: Its Essence and Development (Oxford: Bruno Cassirer Limited, 1951), pp. 38-43.

[10]Samyutta-nikāya, IV, 251-52.

[11] Huston Smith, The Religions of Man (New York: Harper and Brothers, 1958), p. 125.

[12] Udāna 80.

[13] Quoted in Edward Conze, ed., Buddhist Texts Through the Ages (Oxford: Bruno Cassirer, 1954), pp. 99-100.

[14] H. Smith, op. cit., p. 360, footnote 30.

[15] Chang Chung-yuan, Creativity and Taoism (New York: Harper and Row, 1970), p. 30.

[16] Tao Te Ching, Ch. 14.

[17] Ibid., Ch. 4.

[18] D. T. Suzuki, Mysticism: Christian and Buddhist (New York: Harper and Row, 1957), pp. 18-19.

[19] Tao Te Ching, Ch. 25.

[20] Suzuki, op. cit., pp. 76-77.

[21] Ibid., p. 126.

[22] Tillich, op. cit., I, 239.

[23] Ibid., p. 239.

[24] See Robert P. Scharlemann, "Tillich's Method of Correlation: Two Proposed Revisions," in Journal of Religion, Vol. XLVI, No. 1, Part 2, January 1966, pp. 92ff; and Paul Tillich, "Rejoinder," in the same journal, pp. 184ff.

[25] Arend Th. van Leeuwen, Christianity in World History, tr. by H. H. Hoskins (New York: Charles Scribner's Sons, 1964), p. 47.

[26] See the First Hexagram of the I Ching.

[27] van Leeuwen, op. cit., p. 51.

[28] Jacob, op. cit., p. 48.

[29] Ludwig Koehler, <u>Old Testament Theology</u>, tr. by A. S. Todd (Philadelphia: Westminster Press, 1957), p. 41.

[30] Jacob, <u>op</u>. <u>cit</u>., p. 51.

[31] Alan Richardson, <u>A Theological Word Book of the Bible</u> (New York: Macmillan, 1950), p. 91.

[32] van Leeuwen, <u>op</u>. <u>cit</u>., p. 47.

[33] Suzuki, <u>op</u>. <u>cit</u>., p. 82.

[34] Tillich, <u>Systematic Theology</u>, I, 247.

[35] <u>Ta Chuan</u>, Sec. I, Ch. 5.

[36] <u>Ibid</u>., Sec. I, Ch. 11.

[37] <u>Ibid</u>.

[38] For comprehensive illustrations see J. Y. Lee, <u>The Principle of Changes</u>, pp. 48, 117ff.

[39] Fung Yu-lan, <u>A History of Chinese Philosophy</u>, Vol. II (Princeton: Princeton University Press, 1953), p. 442.

[40] <u>Ibid</u>.

[41] Ch'u Chai and Winberg Chai, ed., <u>I Ching: Book of Changes</u>, tr. by James Legge (Secaucus, N.J.: University Books, 1964), pp. xl-xli.

[42] <u>Tao Te Ching</u>, Ch. 42.

[43] Sec. I, Ch. 5.

[44] <u>Ta Chuan</u>, Sec. I, Ch. 5.

[45] Suzuki, <u>op</u>. <u>cit</u>., p. 106.

[46] Chang Chung-yuan interprets the word "ch'ang," which is one of the basic concepts of Taoism as the "all-changing changeless." See his <u>Creativity and Taoism</u> (New York: Julian Press, 1963), p. 127.

[47] J. Y. Lee, The Principle of Changes, p. 65.

[48] Chang Chung-yuan, op. cit., p. 72.

[49] Ibid.

[50] J. Y. Lee, op. cit., p. 64.

[51] John C. Murray, op. cit., p. 11.

[52] Leslie Dewart, The Future of Belief: Theism in a World Come of Age (New York: Herder and Herder, 1966), p. 194.

[53] Thomas W. Ogletree, "A Christological Assessment of Dipolar Theism," in Journal of Religion, Vol. 49 (1967), p. 92.

[54] Norman Pittenger, "Contemporary Trend in North American Theology," Religion in Life, 34 (1965), p. 502.

[55] D. T. Suzuki, On Indian Mahayana Buddhism, ed. by Edward Conze (New York: Harper and Row, 1968), p. 270.

[56] Ibid.

[57] D. T. Suzuki, Mysticism, p. 110.

[58] Ibid., p. 120.

[59] Schubert Ogden, The Reality of God and Other Essays (New York: Harper and Row, 1966), p. 60.

[60] Donald Munro, The Concept of Man in Early China (Stanford: Stanford University Press, 1969), p. 128.

[61] Swami Prabahvananda, The Spiritual Heritage of India (Hollywood: Vedanta Press, 1963), p. 55.

Chapter VIII

[1] Joseph Fletcher, Moral Responsibility: Situation Ethics at Work (Philadelphia: The Westminster Press, 1967), p. 17.

[2]G. E. Moore, _Principia Ethica_ (Cambridge: University Press, 1960), p. 41.

[3]_Ibid._, p. 42.

[4]Joseph Fletcher, _Morals and Medicine_ (Princeton: Princeton University Press, 1954), p. 223.

Chapter IX

[1]William Braden, _The Age of Aquarius_ (Chicago: Quadrangle Books, 1970), p. 178.

[2]Mircea Eliade, _The Two and the One_ (New York: Harper and Row, 1965), p. 95.

[3]Value numbers of yin and yang are based on the outcome of the manipulation of yarrow stalks or coins at the process of divination. These numbers are bases on the lines of hexagrams. See author's _The Principle of Changes_, pp. 249ff.

[4]_Tao Te Ching_, Ch. 40.

[5]_Ibid._, Ch. 15, 37.

[6]W. Braden, _op. cit._, p. 233.

[7]Kissinger addressed to the Sixth Special Session of the U.N. on April 15, 1974.

Chapter X

[1]H. H. Price, "The Problem of Life After Death," _Religious Studies_, III (1968), 447-459.

[2]_I Ching Hsi Tz'u_, Ch. 1.

[3]Paul Tillich, _Systematic Theology_, III (Chicago: University of Chicago Press, 1963), p. 54.

[4]Benoy G. Ray, The Philosophy of Rabindranath Tagore (Calcutta: Progressive Publishers, 1970), p. 81.

[5]From The Gardener, pp. 138-139; Quoted in Ibid., p. 80.

[6]From Lover's Gift and Crossing, Lover's Gift, 43; Quoted in Ibid., p. 81.

[7]Tillich, op. cit., p. 53.

[8]Aubry R. Johnson, The Vitality of the Individual in the Thought of Ancient Israel, 2nd ed. (Cardiff: University of Wales Press, 1964), p. 88.

[9]Lawrence LeShan, "Psychotherapy and the Dying Patient," Death and Dying, ed. by Leonard Pearson (Cleveland: Case Western Reserve University, 1969), p. 30.

[10]Donald Munro, The Concept of Man in Early China (Stanford: Stanford University Press, 1969), p. 128.

[11]Piyadassi Thera, Buddhism (Ceylon: Buddhist Publications Society), p. 50.

[12]Tao Te Ching, Ch. 50.

[13]Edward Conze, Buddhism: Its Essence and Development (New York: Philosophical Library, 1951), pp. 23-24.

[14]The I Ching or Book of Changes: The Richard Wilhelm Translation, rendered into English by Cary F. Baynes, 3rd ed. (Princeton: Princeton University Press, 1967), p. 129.

[15]The I Ching, James Legge Translation (Oxford: Clarendon Press, 1899), p. 85.

[16]Jung Young Lee, Death and Beyond in the Eastern Perspective (New York: Gordon and Breach, 1974), p. 28.

[17]Elisabeth Kübler-Ross, On Death and Dying (New York: Macmillan, 1969), p. 100.

[18]Ta Chuan, Hexagram 23.

[19] J. Y. Lee, op. cit., p. 56.

[20] W. Y. Evans-Wentz, ed., The Tibetan Book of the Dead (London: Oxford University Press, 1960), p. liii.

[21] J. Y. Lee, op. cit., p. 62.

[22] The Tibetan Book of the Dead, p. 102.

[23] See The Tibetan Book of the Dead, pp. 105ff.

[24] The Richard Wilhelm Translation, p. 166.

Chapter XI

[1] See his Foreword in The I Ching or Book of Changes: The Richard Wilhelm Translation.

[2] Max Born, Natural Philosophy of Cause and Chance (New York: Dover Publications, 1964), p. 3.

[3] Ibid.

[4] See his The Roots of Coincidence (New York: Random House, 1972), especially pp. 82ff.

[5] Carl Jung, "On Synchronicity," Man and Time: Papers from the Eranos Yearbooks (New York: Pantheon Books, 1957), p. 209.

[6] Ibid., p. 207.

INDEX

Above, 29, 158

Abraham, 125

Absolute, 62, 64, 66-67, 73, 86, 124, 132, 140

Absolution, 184

Abyss, 38

Acausality, 45, 70, 195

Accident, 196

Acupuncture, 83-105, 107; as anesthesia, 83, 84; clinics, 83; cosmological implications of, 103-105; empirical evidence of, 84-85; philosophy of, 86; promotion of, 83; rules of, 101-104; scientific research of, 84-85; technique, 84, 89, 97, 105; therapy, 83, 84, 85, 86; theory of, 84, 85, 87, 97; with animals, 84

Acupuncturists, 98, 100-101

Adulthood, 181

Air, 169, 171

"All-changing changeless," 137

Americans, 83, 158

Analects, 10, 18, 19

Analogy, 127, 128, 136, 160

Anesthesia, 83

Anger, 88

Anima, 108, 162

Animus, 108, 162

Anti-electron, 48, 71

Antimatter, 71

Anti-particle, 48, 71

Anti-technology, 166

Apocryphas, 24, 91

Appendix, 3 7

April-May, 191

Aquinas, Thomas, 123

Archetypes, 1, 40, 114-121, 145, 179, 193-195; male-female, 109

Aristotle, 123, 157

Armpits, 88, 98

Arms, 96-100

Arousing, 38, 181, 190

Artificiality, 169

Astronomic science, 64

Asymmetry, 163

Ātman, 142

Atoms, 40, 48, 63, 68, 74-78, 81

Attachment, 22, 168, 190; total, 186

August-September, 183

Augustine, 114

Autohypnosis, 84

Automation, 67

Autonomy, 1, 145, 179, 201

Autumn, 89, 184

Axiology, 148

Axis, 136, 138

Background, 52, 55, 109-110, 153, 178, 186

Balance, 76-78, 87, 93, 95, 96, 97, 101, 102, 109, 132

Bamboo, 38

Banquets, 165

Bardo Thödol, 186, 188, 189

Beauty, 57, 205

Becoming, 125, 130, 133-138; creative, 138, 181; process of, 24, 135, 138, 141, 179

"Becoming itself," 132-133

Being, 115, 130, 140; structure of, 130-132, 137; unchanging, 123

"Being itself," 124, 129-130, 137

Below, 29, 158

Chinese, 44, 63; civilization, 60, 85; dictionary, 22; empire, 80; people, 16; philosophy, 63

Ching (classic), 22

Ching (well), 165-166

Ching Tien Shin Wen, 20

Chönyid Bardo, 188

Chou Dynasty, 8, 14, 15, 21

Chou Hsin, 14

Chou I, 9-10, 15; see also the I Ching

Chou Kung, see Tan

Chou Tun-i, 50, 63, 134-135

Christians, 197

Ch'u Chai, 51, 135

Chu Hsi, 63, 91

Chuang Chou, 63

Chung Kua, 39

Church, 159-160

Cinema, 190

Circles, 11

"Circulation-sex organ," 44-97, 100

Classifications, 56

Clear Light of the Void, 186

Climate, 92-93

Closed circuit, 78

Closing, 32-33, 77

Cloth, 6

Club, Psychological, 45

Cognition, 112

Cogwheels, 67

Coincidence, 45, 58, 79, 170, 194-199; meaningful, 45; pure, 194-195

Coins, 177; tossing, 117-118, 145, 166

Cold, 29, 35, 89, 93, 184, 185

Collapse, 41

Color, 22, 38

Commentary, 4

Community, 159-160, 166; global, 160

Competition, 158-159

Complementarity (complementary relationship), 30-31, 32, 49, 52, 69-70, 86, 94, 107, 109, 111-112, 146-148, 159-164, 166, 177, 195-199; principle of, 72-74

"Complementary ethics," 146-148

Complexity, 167-168, 205

Computer, 167, 169; archetypical, 80-81; science, 78-81; technology, 58, 80

Conch-shells, 175

Concubine, 39

Confrontation, 181

Confucius, 2, 10, 17, 18, 19, 20, 21, 28, 150; classics of, 181

Consciousness, 109-115, 119-121, 151-156, 186, 200-201; pure, 127

Constancy, 19, 27-28

Contemplation, 184

Contextual ethics, 145-150

Continuum, 1, 57-58, 92, 161, 174, 177, 178

Contraction, 33, 36, 42, 54

Conze, Edward, 181-182

Cooperation, 158-161

Corinthians, 159

Correlation, 45, 46, 89, 95

Correspondence, 45

Cosmology, 8, 10, 61-62, 103, 117; Chinese, 85-90

Cosmos, 28, 42, 86, 87, 117, 141, 159, 170-172

Counterpart body, 48

Court, 2

Cow, 6

Creativity, 25, 29, 37-38, 63, 110, 133-135, 156, 181, 182, 191, 201

Creator, 124

Fu (Returning), 41, 75-76, 180, 187-188
Fu Hsi, 7, 8, 10, 11, 13, 14, 15, 16, 78-80, 93
Fung Yu-lan, 134-135

Galaxies, 64
Gallbladder, 94, 96-98
Game, 197; mathematical, 194
Gardner, Martin, 79
"Gate Control" Theory, 84
"Gate of life," see "Circulation-sex organ"
Gate-keeper, 39
Genesis, 131
Gentile, 38, 160
Gentle, 38
Geometry, Euclidian, 61
German, 47
Global, 171-172
God, 67, 68, 123-142; Biblical, 129
Godhead, 129
Good, 56-57, 86, 146-150
Good fortune, 7, 74
Gossiping, 39
Govinda, A., 187
Grand Ise Shinto Shrine, 9
Grasses, 88
Great Beginning, 91; see also T'ai Ch'u
Great Change, 91; see also T'ai I
Great Commentary, 23; see also Ta Chuan
Great Dipper, 88
Great Etheral, 92
Great Harmony, 92
Great Light, 185
Great Ultimate, 50-51, 134-135, 161, 176; see also T'ai Chi
Great Ultimate Beginning, 12-13
Guidelines, 202; ethical, 151-154

Hairs, 88
Hallucinations, 115
Han Dynasty, 10, 21, 90, 91
Happiness, 95
Harmony, 87-90, 94, 95, 106, 109, 110-111, 148-150, 157, 158
Hayah, 125, 130
Head, 87, 96-98
Healing, Book of, 106; process, 106
Heat, 94
Heaven, 4, 5, 10, 12, 13, 23, 25, 27, 28, 29, 32, 33, 37-38, 40, 42, 79, 88, 95, 97, 131, 134-135, 150, 170, 179
Heavy, 37
Hebrews, 124, 125, 132, 137, 138; Epistle of, 139
Hegel, 63
Heisenberg, W., 47, 68-70, 71-73, 81
Heng (Penetrating), 19, 156-157
Hermeneutic, 203
Hexagrams, 1-6, 39-43, 74-78, 118-121, 133, 145, 167, 169, 179-192, 201-204; arrangement of, 6, 8, 13, 14, 78-79, 194; authorship of, 8, 13-14; lines of, 25, 100; name of, 1, 2; order of, 6, 79-81; original and consequent, 118-119; texts of, 7, 193; sixty-four, 1, 3, 13, 14, 39, 43, 112, 114, 135; symbols of, 4, 5, 17
Hinduism, 161, 167
Ho T'u, see River Map
Holistic view, 106-107
Hollow, 142
"Hollow organs," see Fu
Hope, 201
Hot, 89, 93

227

Hsi Tz'u Chuan (Commentary on
  Appended Judgments), 5, 135
Hsia Yu, 13
Hsiang Chuan (Commentary on the
  Symbols of Hexagrams), 4
Hsiao Sheng Kua (formation of
  trigrams), 39; see also trigrams
Hsiao T'uan (judgment on lines),
  3, 8
Hsing (forms), 91
Hsu Kua Chuan (Commentary on
  the Sequence of Hexagrams), 6
Husband, 4
"Husband-wife rule," 101, 102
Huxley, A., 169

I (Righteousness), 157
I (Change), 9, 12, 20, 22, 23, 24,
  25, 50, 51, 133, 135, 144,
  168; see also Change
I (Cheek), 118-119
"I am that I am," 125, 129, 137
I Chien (Easy and Simple), 24
I Ching (Book of Change), 1, 3-6,
  9, 14-18, 20-22, 31, 40, 42,
  44, 45, 60, 63, 70-71, 74,
  79-82, 91-92, 105, 108, 113,
  124, 133, 158-171, 174-175,
  177, 179-192, 193-195, 197-
  199, 201-202; as book of healing, 106-107, 115-116, 122;
  authorship of, 7, 15; cosmology
  of, 61-65, 85-90, 203; ethics
  of, 146-157; origin of, 7-16;
  philosophies of, 5, 7, 18, 22-
  43, 69, 73, 203; principles of,
  5, 18, 104-105; science of,
  44, 53; study of, 7, 20, 203-
  205; texts of, 7, 20
I T'ung (Explanations of Change),
  135
I-Wei Chien Tso-tzu, 24, 91

Illness, 93, 117; treatment of,
  96, 97, 98, 103, 104, 107
Illusion, optical, 44
Images, 114-116, 134; see also
  symbols
Imbalance, 87, 93, 94, 98, 101
"Immovable First Mover," 123
Inauthentic, 169
Incarnation, 187
Inconclusive, 49, 52, 108
Increase, 36, 102, 103
Indetermination, principle of,
  47, 68-70
Individuation, 106, 107-108,
  112; creative, 108, 110
Infinite, 112; possibility, 141;
  power, 181
"Ink-blot designs," 119
Innocence, 120-121
Integration, 106, 107-108, 112;
  creative, 108, 110
Intellection, 46, 48, 53, 158
Intension, 34
Interdependence, 32, 40, 52,
  57-58, 66, 94, 102, 104,
  107, 200, 204
"Internal organs," see Ts'ang
Intestine, large, 94, 97-101;
  small, 94, 98, 101
Isaac, 125
"Is-ness," 125, 126, 128-130,
  132-133
"Is-ness itself," 129-130, 132-
  133, 136-138, 141-142
Israel, 125
Issues, ethical, 56-57, 143-157
Isticheit, 129

Jacob, 125
Jacob, Edmond, 125, 131
Japan, 9, 15, 50, 81, 105, 129
Jen (Empathy), 157